ABC GUIDE
MEETING INDIVIDUAL CARE AND SUPPORT NEEDS

Level 3

Mark Walsh

ABC GUIDE MEETING INDIVIDUAL CARE AND SUPPORT NEEDS

Published by Textbook Training *Publishers*

Learning support for health and social care

© Text copyright Mark Walsh 2016

Mark Walsh asserts the moral right to be identified as the author of this work.

All rights reserved.

Also available in this series:

Human Lifespan Development – An ABC Guide
ISBN 978-1533477200

Working in Health and Social Care – An ABC Guide
ISBN 978-1533356024

Anatomy and Physiology – An ABC Guide
ISBN 978-1533356093

Psychological Perspectives – An ABC Guide
ISBN 978-1533082329

Sociological Perspectives – An ABC Guide
ISBN 978-1533356208

HEALTH AND SOCIAL CARE

Introduction

This *ABC Guide to Meeting Individual Care and Support Needs* covers 70 entries that define, discuss and explain a range of concepts, terms and theories that feature in unit 6 of BTEC National Health and Social Care (2016). The *ABC Guide to Meeting Individual Care and Support Needs* has been written to provide learners with a broad ranging resource to support learning within this particular unit.

Unlike a textbook, the ABC Guide is not designed to be read sequentially. You can find and access information about any one entry as the need arises but also follow some links between entries to build up and develop your understanding of a topic area. Try using a particular term as a 'way in' or jumping off point and go from there!

At the end of each entry the *See also* suggestions are used to indicate how the term is connected to other issues, debates and topics within and beyond the unit you are studying. You are encouraged to follow up some of these links and to move between the entries to clarify and deepen your understanding. References are also provided where appropriate and could be followed up as a way of extending your knowledge and understanding if you have a strong interest in a particular topic or issue.

The entries in the ABC Guide cover all 12 of the key content areas of the unit 6 specification of your BTEC National Health and Social Care course. Table 1 that follows on pages 4, 5 and 6 tells you where each of the ABC Guide entries fits into your course.

Mark Walsh

ABC GUIDE MEETING INDIVIDUAL CARE AND SUPPORT NEEDS

Table 1 – Where do the terms fit into unit 6?

Unit 6 Key Content Areas	Concepts	ABC guide page
A1 Promoting equality, diversity and preventing discrimination	Advocacy services	9-11
	Anti-discriminatory practice	14-15
	Care values	27-30
	Discrimination	69-71
	Diversity	72-73
	Equality	80
A2 Skills and personal attributes required for developing relationships with individuals	Care	25
	Care values	27-30
	Conflict / conflict management	61-63
	Observation skills	113-115
	6Cs	131-132
A3 Empathy and establishing trust with individuals	Attachment theory	16-20
	Autonomy	21
	Empathy	76-77
	Resilience	123-125
	Triangle of care	141-142
B1 Ethical issues and approaches	Care values	27-30
	Carers	31-33
	Consequentialism	64-65
	Deontology	68
	Ethical issues	78-79
	Principlism	121-122
	Risk	126-130
	Virtue ethics	143-144

HEALTH AND SOCIAL CARE

Unit 6 Key Content Areas	Concepts	ABC guide page
B2 Legislation and guidance on conflict of interest, balancing resources and minimising risk	Legislation	98-99
	Mental Capacity Act 2005	101-102
	Mental Health Act 2007	103-104
	Risk	126-130
C1 Enabling individuals to overcome challenges	Adult Social Care Outcomes Framework	8
	Clinical audit	34
	Health Action Plans	83-84
	Individual needs	93-95
	NHS Patient Experience Framework	111-112
C2 Promoting personalisation	Personalised care	116-117
	Personalisation	118-120
	Support	137-140
C3 Communication techniques	Braille	22-23
	British Sign Language	24
	Communication approaches	35-40
	Communication boards	41-42
	Communication skills	43-47
	Communication theories	48-54
	Communication technologies	55-56
	Makaton	100

ABC GUIDE MEETING INDIVIDUAL CARE AND SUPPORT NEEDS

Unit 6 Key Content Areas	Concepts	ABC guide page
D1 How agencies work together to meet individual care and support needs	Agencies	12
	Common Assessment Framework (CAF)	57-58
	Education, Health and Care Plan	74
	Healthcare Commissioning	89-90
	Integrated Health and Social Care organisations	96-97
	National Eligibility Criteria (Care Act 2014)	107-109
	National Framework for NHS Continuing Healthcare	110
	Social care commissioning	133-134
D2 Roles and responsibilities of key professionals on multi-disciplinary teams	Allied health professionals	13
	Carers	31-33
	Education professionals	75
	Healthcare professionals	91-92
	Multi-agency working	105
	Multidisciplinary team	106
	Social care workers	135-136
	Voluntary sector workers	145

HEALTH AND SOCIAL CARE

Unit 6 Key Content Areas	Concepts	ABC guide page
D3 Maintaining confidentiality	Care values	27-30
	Confidentiality	59-60
	Health and Social Care Act 2012	86-87
	Health and Social Care Information Centre (HSCIC)	88
D4 Managing information	Care Quality Commission	26
	Data Protection Act 1998	66-67
	Freedom of Information Act 2000	81-82
	Health and Care Professions Council (Codes of practice)	85
	Legislation	98-99
	Mental Capacity Act 2005	101-102
	Mental Health Act 2007	103-104

ABC GUIDE MEETING INDIVIDUAL CARE AND SUPPORT NEEDS

Adult Social Care Outcomes Framework

The Adult Social Care Outcomes Framework (ASCOF) is a government initiative, developed by the Department of Health and local authority bodies, that aims to measure how well adult social care services perform in providing high quality care for vulnerable people in society. It is an example of a policy framework that aims to evaluate how well social care services have been helping individuals to overcome the challenges they face.

The ASCOF is used by local and national social care agencies to establish priorities for social care and support, to measure progress in service provision and to ensure that the effects, or outcomes, of social care provision are measured and reported on.

ASCOF covers four main areas:

- Enhancing quality of life for people with care and support needs
- Delaying and reducing the need for care and support
- Ensuring that people have a positive experience of care and support
- Safeguarding adults whose circumstances make them vulnerable, and protecting them from avoidable harm.

The framework has produced annual results since 2011. These show how well each local authority has performed against the ASCOF standards. This allows people to see how well their own local authority performs and also enables them to compare performance in their own area to the performance of other local authorities.

See also – Adult Social Care; Agencies; Social Care Professionals;

Advocacy services

Advocacy
The act of pleading or arguing in favor of something, such as a cause, policy, or interests o[f] active support of an idea or c[...]

Advocacy is the process of speaking on behalf of someone who is unable to represent their own interests.

Advocacy may be used where a person is too ill or frail, lacks confidence or the social and communication skills to represent their own interests. The aim is to ensure that the individual's rights are respected, that their needs are recognised and any entitlements given. Advocates can be trained (as paid or volunteer workers) or untrained (usually a friend or relative). An advocate must represent the client's views and interests and not simply express their own view.

Advocacy services and opportunities are increasingly regarded as basic facilities that should be offered to all users of care services, but particularly those groups which have historically been less able to express their needs, views and wishes independently. Two main forms of advocacy are used in care settings:
- Citizen advocacy refers to the voluntary involvement of an advocate in the life of somebody with health needs or social care problems. Citizen advocates work alongside service users to represent their interests. Citizen advocacy is quite common in mental health and learning disabilities settings. Citizen advocates usually offer to support and enable patients or clients to identify and communicate their needs and wishes to care professionals or to family members.

- Self-advocacy refers to 'a process whereby service users are encouraged to speak out directly for themselves' (Brandon and Brandon, 1991). Groups of service users tend to promote self-advocacy and provide training and support to enable members to develop the skills and confidence to speak up for themselves.

Advocacy services typically help people to:

- identify and obtain information relevant to themselves and their care or support
- understand and explore the choices and options they have in relation to care and other issues affecting their health or personal circumstances.
- think through and make decisions about issues that affect some aspect of their life
- obtain and defend their rights
- raise issues and make complaints about decisions that affect them or about the way care services operate and affect them.

Many local authorities and NHS Trusts fund advocacy services to ensure that service users rights are protected and that they have a voice and way of being heard in what can be large organisations and a complex care system. Similarly, there are many examples of advocacy services provided by voluntary sector groups / charities to support and provide a voice on the specific issues that affect their members or service user group. People with learning disabilities, mental health problems, physical disabilities and dementia, as well as members of families and informal carers who support them, have a long history of using advocacy services. These groups have tended to experience difficulty in overcoming the power imbalance that exists in their relationships with care professionals and benefit from having independent support to get their voice heard and their wishes met.

A legal or statutory right to advocacy services has been introduced through a number of recent laws. The Mental Capacity Act (2005) introduced Independent Mental Capacity Advocates (IMCAs) to support people who lack mental capacity to make or understand decisions that affect them and who has nobody else to represent their interests when decisions need to be made. An IMCA must be appointed if an NHS body or local authority proposes serious medical treatment or to house or rehouse a person lacking the mental capacity to make a decision about this themselves. Similarly, the Care Act (2014) and the Mental Health Act (2007) have introduced new statutory rights to advocacy for people who have substantial difficulty in participating in assessments of their needs or decisions about care, support or treatment that affect them.

See also – Anti-discriminatory practice; Care values; Discrimination; Diversity; Equality; Personalisation; Support.

ABC GUIDE MEETING INDIVIDUAL CARE AND SUPPORT NEEDS

Agencies

The term 'agency' is generally used in the social care sector to refer to an organisation, such as a local authority or an independent sector (voluntary or private) organisation that provides social care or support services. It is also used in a related but broader way to refer to a group of organisations – such as the local authority, police, probation service, voluntary group and community health services - working together in a collaborative way. The agencies involved in this kind of work often refer to it as multi-agency working

Social workers and care managers are most likely to refer to the 'agency' they work for. Healthcare practitioners tend not to use the term 'agency' when referring to their employer unless they are employed on a part-time, temporary basis through a private sector (commercial) staffing agency. This use of the term agency is distinct from the way it is used by social care professionals to refer to their employing organisation.

See also – Common Assessment Framework (CAF); Education, Health and Care Plan; Healthcare commissioning; Multi-agency working; National Eligibility Criteria; National Framework for NHS Continuing Healthcare; Voluntary sector.

Allied health professionals

Allied health professionals are health care practitioners who are specifically trained to provide a specialist form of health care or treatment other than nursing or medicine. This group of practitioners include:

- Podiatrists (feet)
- Dieticians (nutrition / diet)
- Music Therapists
- Physiotherapists
- Diagnostic and therapeutic radiographers (X-rays)
- Speech and language therapists
- Occupational therapists

Allied health professionals generally have to complete a degree or diploma to become a registered practitioner. Most allied health professions are required to join a register of qualified practitioners that is maintained and regulated by the Health and Care Professions Council (HCPC).

Allied health professionals are often part of a health or social care team – and may even be the manager or lead practitioner in a multi-disciplinary team - but also carry their own caseloads of patients or clients referred to them by other professionals. An AHP may work in a hospital, an outpatient clinic, care home or in a community setting such as a GP practice / health centre, a service user's home, a school, college or workplace, for example.

See also – HCPC (codes of practice); Education professionals; Healthcare professionals; Multi-disciplinary team; Multi-agency working; Social care professionals; Voluntary sector workers.

ABC GUIDE MEETING INDIVIDUAL CARE AND SUPPORT NEEDS

Anti-discriminatory practice

Anti-discriminatory practice is an approach to care work that explicitly seeks to tackle unfair discrimination as a way of promoting the rights and equality of each person using care services. Unfair discrimination occurs when individuals or groups of people are treated differently, unequally and unfairly in comparison to others. For example, an employer who refused to interview candidates under the age of 25 for a nursery manager post saying 'in my experience, younger people are not good at accepting responsibility', would be treating young people in an unfair and discriminatory way.

All users of care services should be treated fairly and equally. However, anti-discriminatory practice does not just mean treating everybody the same. It also means challenging and reducing any form of unfair discrimination that might be experienced by service users. Care practitioners who take an anti-discriminatory approach are:
- aware of the different forms of unfair discrimination that can occur in care settings
- sensitive to the diversity and cultural needs of each individual for whom they provide care
- prepared to actively challenge and try to reduce the unfair discrimination experienced by service users

HEALTH AND SOCIAL CARE

Anti-discriminatory practice is also seen as a general perspective, and part of a 'diversity approach' that pays attention to the realities of discrimination and oppression, within social work. From this perspective, reducing individual and institutional discrimination is more than 'political correctness'. It aims to support service users, assist them in tackling discrimination in their lives as well as challenging instances of discrimination. Anti-discriminatory practice now tends to be incorporated into an ant-oppressive practice approach that focuses broadly on differences in power between individuals, groups and a range of agencies involved in health and social care provision.

See also – Advocacy; Autonomy; Discrimination; Diversity; Equality.

Attachment theory

The concept of attachment refers to a biologically-based drive in an infant to form an enduring emotional bond with a caregiver, usually their mother, that keeps them safe and cared for while they are too young to take care of themselves. Attachment theory builds on this concept and a range of evidence about the ways attachment impacts on later development and relationships.

Attachment theories are now an important part of health and social care practice. They are particularly relevant to work with children and families in distress and people whose behavioural and mental health problems are rooted in childhood insecurities and subsequent relationship difficulties.

John Bowlby's trilogy of books entitled *Attachment and Loss* (1969, 1973, 1980) brought the concept of attachment, and attachment theory more generally, to the attention of health and social care practitioners. He was a British psychoanalyst who saw first-hand the destructive impact of mother-child separations in post-World War 2 England. Bowlby saw attachment as a feature of human evolution in which a relatively vulnerable child sought protection from his or her mother. The absence or loss of a mother or reliable caregiver had a negative impact on the child's social and emotional development.

This is because, according to Bowlby, every child is motivated to achieve and maintain a sense of security – a feeling of being safe and looked after. When a child feels secure, the attachment system is deactivated and the exploratory system takes over. The availability and responsiveness of the child's mother or caregiver is critical to this process.

Bowlby argued that through repeated attachment experiences, a child develops an 'internal working model' of how their interactions with their mother (or caregiver) will typically play out. This has a profound effect on their subsequent attachment behaviour

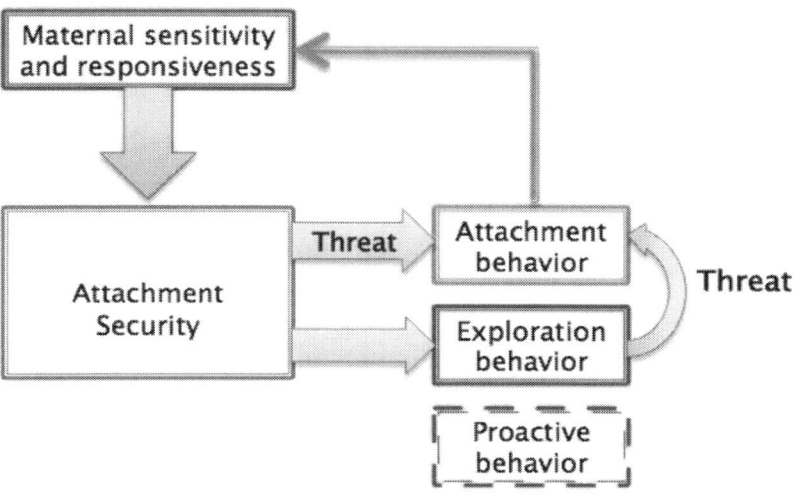

Figure 1 – An illustration of the attachment process

Mary Ainsworth (1978), a colleague of John Bowlby, developed a laboratory experiment called the 'strange situation' to explore and test the concept of attachment. She was particularly interested in individual differences in the quality of mother-infant attachment. The strange situation is a twenty-minute procedure involving infants aged twelve to eighteen months and their mothers entering a room full of toys. They are observed through a one-way mirror by a psychologist who is looking at their reactions when a sequence of eight separations and reunions occur. The first separation lasts for on thirty seconds. The rest last for up to three minutes. Based on how they react, the infant is classed as either securely attached or into one of three insecurely attached categories:

- Securely attached infants show interest in the toys when the mother is in the room. Some show mild to moderate distress during separation. Importantly, the securely attached infants sought direct contact with their mother during the reunions. Any distress is quickly soothed by the mother. According to Ainsworth, this pattern of behaviour shows the child feels secure because they know their mother is available and will respond to their attachment needs.
- Insecurely attached infants feel uncertain and emotionally insecure about their mother's availability and responsiveness to their attachment needs. In the strange situation they show greater interest in the toys than their mother and are not really distressed during separations. Those who have an avoidant attachment turn away when reunited with their mothers. By contrast, infants who have a 'resistant attachment' don't really play with the toys much when their mother is present and become much more distressed when separated. They do seek out their mother on reunion but resist attempts to calm and sooth them. Ainsworth argues that these children are overly dependent and are trying to maximise their mother's attention because they are uncertain about her emotional availability and responsiveness.

Disorganised attachment is the final type of attachment relationship. Infants who have a disorganised attachment don't display a consistent strategy for dealing with attachment and separation and may seem fearful of their mother / parent.

HEALTH AND SOCIAL CARE

This pattern of attachment is more likely to be found in children who have experienced abuse or whose mothers have emotional difficulties themselves and do not respond to their children in an appropriate and consistent way. In these circumstances, the infant or child can't find a consistent way of dealing with their parent's erratic or frightening behaviour.

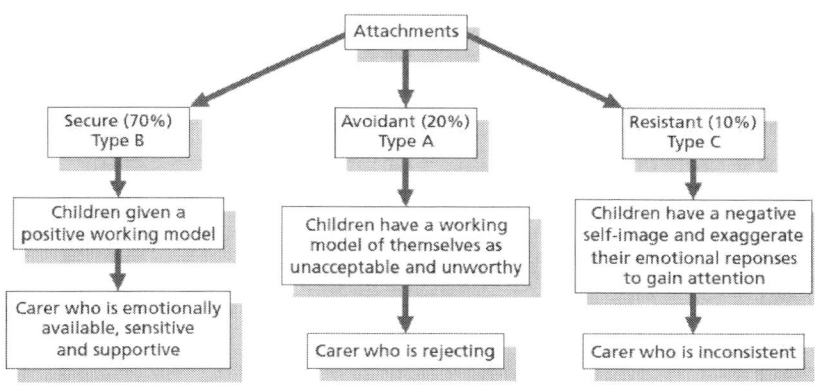

Figure 2 – A summary of Ainsworth's types of normal attachment

John Bowlby (1989) argued that secure attachment equips an infant with the emotional capacity to understand others and to form effective relationships at various points in their life. The capacity for attachment, based on an individual's first relationship with their parent(s) or caregivers, is seen as providing a 'blueprint' for later social and emotional development. Consequently, poor or faulty attachment may lead to deep feelings of insecurity and difficulties in forming and maintaining relationships in later life.

ABC GUIDE MEETING INDIVIDUAL CARE AND SUPPORT NEEDS

Attachment is an issue that interests early years and education workers, health and social care workers supporting children and families and psychologists, counsellors and psychotherapists working with people across the lifespan. In mental health settings, attachment issues are particularly important when working with people experiencing relationship difficulties and those who have been diagnosed with a personality disorder.

See also – Autonomy; Empathy; Resilience.

References
Ainsworth, M.D., Blehar, M.C., Waters, E., and Wall, S. (1978), *Patterns of attachment: Assessed in the strange situation and at home*, New Jersey, LEA.
Bowlby J. (1969, 1973, 1980) *Attachment and Loss*, New York: Basic Books
Bowlby J. (1989) *A Secure Base*, Routledge

Autonomy

Autonomy is a philosophical idea or concept that refers to the right to be self-governing. That is, a person who has 'autonomy' is free and capable of making decisions for themselves.

In health and social care settings, all service users are assumed to be autonomous (to have autonomy) unless they lack the mental capacity to understand and make decisions for themselves. People who have dementia, some people with mental health problems and some people with learning disabilities or a neurological (brain-based) condition, may not have the mental capacity to be autonomous.

Respect for the autonomy of each individual service user is the foundation of 'informed consent'. Care, treatment or other interventions can only proceed if the person understands what is being proposed and agrees to this. Because they have autonomy, the person has the right to decline or refuse treatment, care or intervention – even in situations where qualified and experienced practitioners recommend or advise them to accept it.

Acknowledging and respecting each individual's right to autonomy should also have a major effect on the way health and social care practitioners form relationships and interact with service users. Accepting an individual as an autonomous person means that they are an equal and that any care or therapeutic relationship with them is a partnership. It isn't acceptable for a health or social care worker to use their professional expertise and position to disempower or impose decisions on an autonomous person. There are some exceptions to this – such as where the individual lacks mental capacity – but it is generally good professional practice to ensure everything is done to respect an individual's autonomy.

See also – Attachment; Consequentialism; Deontology; Empathy; Mental Capacity Act 2005; Resilience.

ABC GUIDE MEETING INDIVIDUAL CARE AND SUPPORT NEEDS

Braille

Braille is a communication system developed for, and used by, people who are blind or have a significant degree of visual impairment. It is named after Louis Braille, a Frenchman who lost his sight in an accident when he was fifteen years of age.

The Braille language system is based on small rectangular blocks (cells) that contain six bumps (raised dots) that can be felt by the reader's fingers. A dot may be raised in any one of the six positions to form sixty-four possible combinations. The arrangement of the raised dots in each cell allows the reader to distinguish one character from another. A single cell can be used to represent an alphabet letter, number, punctuation mark, or a whole word. Braille texts can also include embossed illustrations and graphs with the lines either solid or made of series of dots, arrows, bullets that are larger than braille dots, for example.

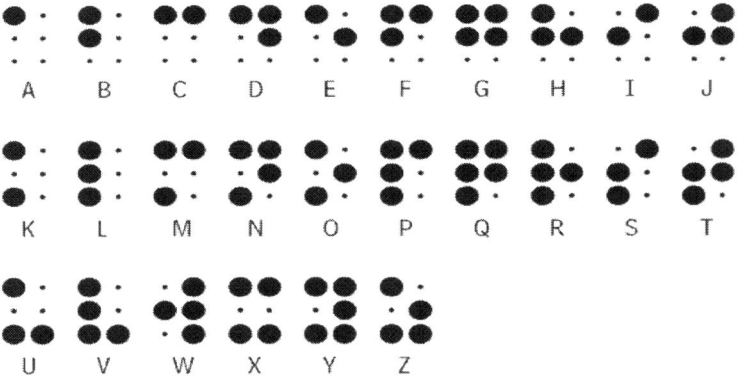

Figure 3 – An illustration of the braille alphabet

HEALTH AND SOCIAL CARE

Traditionally, braille has been produced and read from embossed paper. However, the braille system has also tried keep up with and make use of information technology (computers and printers). Braille-users can now use computer screens with refreshable braille displays and can print out information in braille using a computer / printer with a braille embosser.

There are somewhere between 15,000 and 20,000 braille users in the UK at present. Braille is now less attractive to younger blind and visually impaired people who are tending to make more use of screen-reader software available for most computers, tablets and other electronic devices.

See also – British Sign Language; Communication approaches; Communication boards; Communication skills; Makaton.

ABC GUIDE MEETING INDIVIDUAL CARE AND SUPPORT NEEDS

British Sign Language

British Sign Language (BSL) is a communication system, or form of language, used by approximately 125,000 deaf adults and 20000 children in the United Kingdom. In addition, the partners, families, friends and colleagues of deaf BL users may also learn and use signs to ensure they are able to communicate in an inclusive, accessible way. You may also have seen BSL on some television programmes especially BBC and Channel Four) and being used by official signers at major events (e.g festivals and concerts) in the UK to ensure that deaf people can understand what is going on and being said.

BSL users move their hands, body, face and head to create 'signs' that communicate words or meaning. The shapes made and the position of a person's hands can be used to express words or phrases. There is also a BSL fingerspelling alphabet in addition to the wide range of signs (see www.bslsignbank.ucl.ac.uk) available to learn and use. Like spoken language, BSL also has regional dialects and examples of words that are specific to a particular place. For example, some of the signs that are used in Scotland may not be used – or understood – in other parts of the UK.

BSL is quite widely used in educational settings attended by deaf children, teenagers and adults. Many health and social care organisations also ensure staff trained in BSL are available to support, and communicate with, BSL users. Online and college-based courses make learning BSL accessible to all health and social care workers and students.

See also – Braille; Communication boards; Communication skills; Makaton.

HEALTH AND SOCIAL CARE

Care

Care is a broad, wide-ranging term that is generally used to describe giving or providing a service that aims to meet an individual's immediate health care, developmental, social support or emotional needs or their need for safeguarding and protection.

Care is often distinguished from 'support'. Where this happens, care is seen as deliberate, direct and typically practical or physical intervention (providing care) in ways that have tangible and immediate outcomes. In this sense, 'personal care' refers to forms of active, practical assistance relating to washing, dressing or helping a person to use the toilet or meet their intimate care needs. By comparison, 'support' refers to more indirect forms of assistance or help. Support is associated with offering forms of social and emotional assistance, typically through a close, empathic relationship that respects and empowers the individual to meet their own needs as much as they are able to.

Figure 4 – Care tends to be associated with health, illness and infirmity issues

See also – Autonomy; Support.

ABC GUIDE MEETING INDIVIDUAL CARE AND SUPPORT NEEDS

Care Quality Commission (codes of practice)

The Care Quality Commission (CQC) is an independent regulatory body responsible for inspecting and regulating standards of health and adult social care services in England. The Health and Social Care Act 2008 requires the CQC to publish a code of practice about best practice for obtaining, handling, using and disclosing confidential personal information.

The code of practice is used by CQC to develop policies, processes and training on information handling and management issues. It also provides people who use services with guidance on best practice principles and the standards they can expect CQC to follow in their handling and use of confidential personal information. The CQC code of practice on confidential personal information is necessary because CQC have powers to enter care premises where they can access, obtain and remove personal information related to residents or service users.

See also – Confidentiality; Disability Discrimination Act 1998; HCPC (codes of practice).

References
www.cqc.org.uk

Care values

Care values are fundamental beliefs about the right or correct way of treating service users.

The 'care value base' is an important but slightly confusing concept that is widely used in the fields of health, social care and early years. The Care Sector Consortium, a body responsible for developing National Vocational Qualifications (NVQs), first used the term 'care value base' in 1992. It was used to describe a set of values and principles that were thought to be relevant and common to the work of all health and social care practitioners. The notion of a 'care value base' identified the values and principles that could be used as an ethical guide to decision-making and practice in health, social care and early years settings. This particular care value base covered five main areas of care practice:

- Promoting anti-discriminatory practice
- Maintaining confidentiality
- Promoting and supporting individual's rights
- Acknowledging individuals' personal beliefs and identity
- Promoting effective communication.

These original elements of the 'care value base' are widely recognised and supported by health, social care and early years practitioners. However, whilst many care practitioners may subscribe to these values and try to put them into practice in their work with service users everyday, they may not necessarily think that they are applying the so-called 'care value base'!

'Care value base' is a phrase that is most likely to be recognised by NVQ-qualified care practitioners. Registered care practitioners (such as registered nurses, occupational therapists and registered medical practitioners) who have undertaken a professional care training, are more likely to see these care values as being part of their professions' code of ethics, code of conduct or code of practice. These codes are documents that are developed and issued by the regulatory body of each registered care profession. They lay down the 'rules' for their registered practitioners and provide guidance on what is 'best practice'.

Figure 5 – All care workers have a responsibility to uphold and apply care values in their work with service users.

Professional codes of ethics, conduct and practice may incorporate and express basically the same values as the 'care value base'. However, they often do so in ways that are specific to the care profession that they refer to. For example, the registered nurse's code of professional conduct is slightly different to that of occupational therapists.

Despite this, they both incorporate and apply the fundamentals of the care value base to their areas of care practice. Referring to the *value bases of care* instead of the care value base is a way of recognising the slight differences that occur. Ultimately, it is true to say that care practitioners in general tend to be committed to basing their practice on a set of values and principles. There are a number of reasons for this.

Why do we need and use care values?

The United Kingdom is a diverse, multi-cultural society. As a result, health, social care and early years practitioners come into contact with a very broad range of people who experience an array of differing care needs and problems. No two service users are the same and nobody has exactly the same care needs as another person. Care workers must find ways of acknowledging and responding to the diversity that service users' embody whilst also ensuring that everybody receives a high standard of care based on a respectful, positive and empowering care relationship. How can care practitioners achieve this difficult goal of acknowledging difference and particular needs whilst also treating people equally and fairly? The answer is by applying care values.

In essence, the value bases of care provide necessary guidance because what constitutes 'good practice' can't be assumed and shouldn't have to be thought out by individual care practitioners every time they meet a new service user or have to respond to a new care situation. The value bases of care provide clear guidance on how to provide high quality care to all service users on a consistent basis. They protect both the service user (from poor quality care, neglect and mistreatment) and set out positive principles for care workers to follow in their pursuit of 'good practice'.

Care values and principles in practice

Millar (2015) suggests that the 'care value base' consists of care principles that are derived from two main care values that are at the heart of care practice. These values are:
- Respect for the worth and dignity of every individual
- According social justice and promoting the health and social welfare of every individual

The value of respect for the worth of every individual involves accepting and treating every person as worthy and important in their own right 'simply because that person is a person' (Millar 1996:16). The value of according social justice and promoting the social welfare of every individual is concerned with ensuring that people receive fair and correct treatment in society. The aim is to maximise each person's wellbeing, health experience and life opportunities. These fundamental care values can be put into practice through the care principles of:

- Promoting equality in care practice
- Respecting difference
- Promoting individual's rights
- Promoting choice and empowerment
- Maintaining confidentiality and privacy
- Promoting anti-discriminatory practice

See also – Confidentiality; Consequentialism; Deontology; Ethical issues; Principlism.
References
Millar, J (2015) *Care in Practice*, Hodder

HEALTH AND SOCIAL CARE

Carers

A carer is a person who looks after a partner, relative or friend who is ill or disabled. Carers are also sometimes referred to as 'informal carers' to distinguish them from professional, employed or 'formal' care practitioners (such as doctors, nurses, social workers, care assistants, for example).

According to the 2011 Census there are approximately 6.5 million carers in the UK. The care provided by unpaid carers has been estimated as being worth £119bn per year – more than the total spending on NHS services in England. Being a carer usually comes with a significant workload and often reduces a person's social life and their career and personal development opportunities. Carers UK, a voluntary sector organisation supporting and representing carers in the UK, state that:

> According to the Personal Social Services Survey of Adult Carers in England 2014-15, over a third of carers (38%) are caring for over 100 hours a week. 13.5% of carers care for 19 hours or less a week; 15% care for between 20 and 49 hours a week and almost 14% care for between 50 and 100 hours a week.

Many people become carers unexpectedly because they feel a sense of duty or obligation towards their partner, a relative or a friend. Whilst many carers take on this role willingly, it can also be a difficult thing to do and tends to alter a person's relationship with the person they support or care for. It can be difficult, for example, if a person is working full-time, also caring for young children or have to travel a long distance to provide regular care and support.

The type and amount of care provided by carers varies a great deal. According to the NHS Information Centre Survey of Carers in Households:

- 82% provide practical help such as preparing meals, doing laundry or shopping.
- 76% keep an eye on the person they care for
- 68% keep them company
- 62% take the person they care for out
- 49% help the person they care for with financial matters
- 47% help the person they care for deal with care services and benefits
- 38% help with aspects of personal care such as washing and using the toilet
- 38% provide physical help

Carers are typically unpaid and untrained for the roles they take on, though a carer may receive training to carry out specific procedures relating to medication management, the use of adaptations or equipment, mobility support or personal care provision. Carers are now entitled to an assessment of their own needs and the creation of a plan which can lead to the provision of support to enable them to perform their caring role. This is an important development as caring can have a major impact on a person's physical and mental health, their finances and their opportunities to work.

The role and contribution of carers to the provision of health and social care services is increasingly being recognised though many carers still complain of feeling isolated and unsupported. The contribution that carers make to the overall provision of care is forecast to increase as a result of an ageing and growing UK population and changes in the focus of mainstream health and social care services.

Carers UK estimates that there will be a 40% rise in the number of carers needed by 2037 – an extra 2.6 million carers, meaning the carer population in the UK will reach 9 million.

Figure 6 – Carers often find their career and job opportunities are damaged or limited by their unpaid caring responsibilities.

See also – Care; Support; National Eligibility Criteria; Voluntary sector

References
Carers UK (2015) *Policy Briefing – Facts about carers*, www.carersuk.org
NHS Information Centre for Health and Social Care (2010), Survey of Carers in Households 2009/10

Clinical audit

Clinical audit is "a quality improvement process that seeks to improve patient care and outcomes through systematic review of care against explicit criteria and the implementation of change" (NICE, 2002). The aim of clinical audit is to check or assess whether what is currently being done meets expected standards of best practice and/or could be changed to achieve improvements.

Clinical audit is now well established and is a key part of the quality management process in health and social care organisations. A number of different types of audit exist in the health and social care field. These include:

- *Standards-based audits* which involves defining standards, collecting data to measure current practice against those standards, and implementing any changes deemed necessary.
- *Critical incident / adverse event audits* are used to review incidents in the care setting or in clinical practice that have caused concern or from which there was an unexpected outcome. A multidisciplinary team discussion is held to reflect upon the way the team functioned and to learn for the future.

Clinical audits are an important way of monitoring standards of practice and care provision in health and social care settings. This helps to identify any problems or deficiencies early and also promotes continuous improvement to achieve and sustain best practice standards.

See also – Legislation
References
National Institute for Clinical Excellence, *Principles of Best Practice in Clinical Audit 2002*. NICE

Communication approaches

Effective communication is a core part of health and social care work. Health and social care workers need to develop and use a range of communication skills and techniques in their day to day practise with service users. The communication approach that a practitioner uses in their work depends on a number of factors including:

- the age, characteristics, abilities and needs of the people they care for or support (children, adults, older people, people with learning disabilities, dementia or mental health problems, for example)
- the type of care and support needs an individual has and the impact of these on their communication abilities (physical, intellectual, emotional / psychological, for example)
- the purpose and goals of the care setting and the service being provided (emergency care, mental health assessment or rehabilitation, therapeutic or supported living, for example).

Each of these factors, as well as their training and previous experience, can affect a health and social care worker's choice of communication approach. In practice, a practitioner is likely to use one or more of the following communication approaches:

1. A humanistic, person-centred approach
The humanistic perspective adopts an holistic approach to human experience. It began to influence health and social care practitioners from the mid-twentieth century onwards, largely because of its person-centred approach. Abraham Maslow (1908 – 1970) and Carl Rogers (1902 – 1987), both American psychologists, are now seen as the pioneers of this perspective.

The strengths and limitations of the humanistic approach to communication are summarised in the table below.

Strengths	Limitations
1. Recognises that the complexity of human emotions and relationships affects the way people communicate, develop and behave.	1. Based on relatively vague, unscientific concepts that can't be tested easily. The language of humanism (e.g unconditional positive regard') can also be difficult for some people to understand and use.
2. It encourages users to accept and listen to others unconditionally, promoting trust and encouraging equality in relationships.	2. Encourages people to focus on self-fulfilment and perfecting themselves – it can be seen as narcissistic or self-centred.
3. Sees people as having choices and being capable of resolving their own problems in a positive, individual way.	3. Focuses on the individual rather than on the influence of others or their broader social or cultural surroundings.
4. The ideas and concepts of the humanistic perspective (active listening, empathy, acceptance, genuineness) are flexible and can be applied widely in health and social care settings.	4. Person-centred communication is flexible and useful for short-term interventions but isn't based on a more structured, therapeutic approach unlike psychodynamic and cognitive approaches.
5. The humanistic approach focuses on an individual's current difficulties as they understand them from their own perspective.	5. Humanistic psychology ignores the unconscious – it recognises only those thoughts and behaviours that people are aware of.

2. A behavioural approach

The behavioural approach to communication focuses on behaviour that can be observed. It is sometimes also known as 'learning theory' because its basic focus is on the way that human beings learn and the impact this has on their behaviour and relationships. Ivan Pavlov (1849-1936), a Russian physiologist, and B.F Skinner (1904-1990), an American psychologist, are the theorists most closely associated with the behaviourist perspective.

The strengths and limitations of the behaviourist approach to communication are summarized in the table below.

Strengths	Limitations
1. The behaviourist approach has been widely used to successfully modify and motivate behaviour change in people of all ages. It is easy to understand and doesn't require complex language skills.	1. Behaviourism reduces human behaviour to a simple stimulus-response level. This fails to take into account what people think and feel and wider cultural and environmental influences on behaviour.
2. Behavioural assessment and treatment is relatively quick, inexpensive and solution-focused.	2. Some care workers and psychologists are critical of behaviourism for being manipulative and for not addressing the underlying causes of an individual's problems.
3. Changes in behaviour can be easily measured, monitored and observed.	3. Behavioural techniques work well in controlled environments. They have a more limited application to the real-world behaviour of human beings.

3. A cognitive approach

The cognitive approach sees human beings as information-processors and compares human mental processes to software running on a computer (the brain). The cognitive perspective rose to prominence in the late 1950's, challenging the narrow focus that behaviourism had on observable behaviour. Cognitive psychologists believed that internal mental processes (thinking and memory) play an important part in human communication. Specialist counsellors and therapists using forms of cognitive therapy, doctors, nurses and other health care practitioners and social care workers also incorporate cognitive techniques into their relationship-building and intervention strategies.

The strengths and limitations of the cognitive approach to communication are summarized in the table below.

Strengths	Limitations
1. Recognises that influences on human behaviour and communication are broader and more complex than simple stimulus-response behavioural factors.	1. Ignores the influence of biology, emotions, consciousness and free will on human communication and behaviour.
2. Shows how mental processes and the brain play a key part in the way people communicate and behave.	2. Doesn't recognise the role of the unconscious and early experiences in understanding an individual's communication and behaviour.
3. Sees the person as making some active choices in what they communicate and how they behave.	3. Ignores the human experience of emotions and their impact on communication, behaviour and development.
4. The cognitive approach can be applied quite widely in the health and social care field.	4. It is reductionist and deterministic, suggesting that complex human psychological processes and experiences can be explained largely in terms of brain functioning.

4. A psychodynamic approach

The psychodynamic perspective focuses on the deep, inner psychological aspects of human development and relationships. It is strongly associated with the work of Sigmund Freud (1856 - 1939) on the development of personality and the treatment of 'abnormal' behaviour. The psychodynamic perspective suggests that unconscious forces and conflicts motivate behaviour and can affect communication. It suggests that they are driven by memories, feelings and past experiences and the way the unconscious mind works.

The strengths and limitations of the psychodynamic approach to communication are summarized in the table below.

Strengths	Limitations
1. Psychodynamic communication is effective with certain types of people (articulate, introspective) and certain types of disorders (anxiety-based, linked to attachments and early experiences).	1. Psychodynamic therapies tend to focus on past experiences rather than the current difficulties a person faces.
2. Psychodynamic communication provides a way of seeking out the root causes of people's problems and tries to resolve them.	2. Digging deeply into a person's problems and past experiences can produce more distress (making the person feel worse) before a solution is found and symptoms are relieved.
3. The psychodynamic approach can be used with individuals or groups and is good at giving people insight into their thinking and problems.	3. Psychodynamic treatment is costly and time-consuming and requires a specially trained therapist.

5. A social approach

Social approaches to communication tend to focus on observing and interpreting the interactions of people in groups and one-to-one situations. However, the presence of one or more observers may skew or change the way people interact as if they feel 'watched'. Group situations can also be artificial in the sense that they contain people who have similar characteristics (e.g depression diagnoses) and who may relate differently in groups compared to everyday situations. Practitioners who use social approaches to communication tend to be conscious of cultural issues that may affect communication and seek to acknowledge and respect diversity in an inclusive way.

> ***See also*** – Anti-discriminatory practice; Communication skills; Communication technologies; Diversity; Equality.

Communication boards

Communication boards are specially designed pieces of equipment that are used by people with speech and language impairments. Their purpose is to make language (in the form of photographs, pictures, words and phrases and symbols / shapes) visible and accessible to people who otherwise lack effective verbal communication skills.

Figure 7 – An example of a communication board

Communication board are generally developed to meet a particular individual's communication and language development needs. A person may use multiple boards to learn and express specific and generic vocabulary. It is common for a person who uses communication boards to use them alongside other forms of communication such as British Sign Language, limited speech or Makaton, for example.

Communication boards are commonly used by people who have suffered a stroke or other brain injury, by people with autism and learning disabilities and in some dementia care settings where a person is losing their word-finding and expression abilities. They provide a very adaptable, personalised means of communication that can be used and understood by diverse by children, young people and adults.

> *See also* – Braille; British Sign Language; Communication skills; Communication Technologies; Makaton

Communication skills

Communication is the act of transferring information through verbal messages, written words, visual symbols or subtle non-verbal signals and body language. Health and social care workers need to develop and use a variety of communication skills to interact with service users, colleagues and other people whom they come into contact with in their work roles. These include:

- Spoken or verbal communication skills
- Non-verbal communication skills
- Written communication skills
- Visualisation skills (e.g to create and understand charts, graphs, maps, logos and other visual 'messages')

Verbal communication skills

Verbal communication is based on the use of an oral or spoken language. To communicate verbally a person needs to understand a vocabulary of words and a set of conventions – a grammar – that tells them how to put the words together. Verbal communication occurs when one person speaks and at least one other listens to – and understands – what is being said.

Talking with service users, their relatives and with colleagues is such an everyday activity for health and social care workers that most people aren't aware of, or particularly concerned about, *how* they are speaking when they are doing this. However, health and social care workers do need to understand how they can adapt their verbal communication skills when:

- responding to questions asked by people who use services, their families and friends
- responding to the worries, concerns and distress of people who use care services

- asking questions during assessments or when they are reviewing progress
- running or making contributions to team meetings
- breaking bad news and providing support to people
- communicating with people who have specific hearing, visual or speech impairments or who have a limited ability to use and understand English
- working with colleagues and care professionals from other agencies and professional backgrounds

A number of features of speech can affect the quality and effectiveness of verbal communication. These include the clarity, volume, pace, tone and pitch of a person's voice. For example, it isn't a good idea to shout or to talk so loudly that the other person thinks you are shouting. This type of behaviour is unprofessional and is likely to draw attention away from what is being said as people focus more on how it is being said. They focus on the shouting not on what is being said making communication ineffective. Mumbling, speaking too fast, failing to complete sentences and using a hostile or aggressive tone also makes communication less effective. A health and social care worker's speech should be clear, unambiguous and paced to suit the listener. Speaking in a measured, direct and clear way enables the listener to hear and understand what is being said. Health and social care workers who use a relaxed, encouraging and friendly tone of voice are also able to convey warmth, sincerity and respect for the listener.

Non-verbal communication

We don't have to talk to communicate with other people. As we will see, 'body language', art, drama and music, as well as specialist techniques such as signing, are all non-verbal methods of communication that are used within care settings. Important features of non-verbal communication include posture,

Posture

This term refers to the way that a person sits or stands. People tend to 'read' another person's posture in order to interpret their 'attitude' and feelings. For example, somebody who is sitting or standing in a very upright, stiff way may be seen as being 'tense' or 'serious' in their attitude. 'Closed' postures, where a person has their arms or legs (or both) crossed, tend to suggest defensiveness and tension. 'Open' postures, where the person has their arms loose or 'open' and leans forward slightly, tend to indicate that the person is 'relaxed' and 'comfortable'.

Health and social care workers can use their understanding of postural 'messages' to read a person's mood and feelings. This may be important and revealing during assessment interviews and in one-to-one counselling sessions. However, it is always best to check your 'reading' of a person's postural 'message' with them, by sensitively asking them a question about how they are feeling, to avoid making false interpretations or reading too much into how they are standing or sitting.

Facial expression

The human face is very expressive and is an important source of non-verbal communication. A person's facial expression typically reveals their feelings. However, many people can control their facial expression to disguise their true feelings and present what they believe is a socially acceptable 'face'.

When we 'read' a person's facial expression we look at their:
- Eyes – are the pupils dilated (large) or contracted (small)? Large, dilated pupils tend to suggest 'interest' or excitement.
- Skin colour – Is the person blushing or sweating?
- Mouth – Is the person smiling or frowning? Is the person's mouth dry?
- Facial muscles – Are the muscles in the face tight or relaxed?

Different facial expressions involve very subtle changes in each of these features. Nevertheless, people make use of a very wide range of facial expressions and become very good at 'reading' other people's non-verbal 'messages' in this way.

Proximity and touch
Proximity refers to the physical closeness between people during interactions. Another phrase that is sometimes used instead of proximity is 'personal space'. The amount of personal space that a person needs during an interaction tends to depend on their cultural background, upbringing and the type of relationship that they have with the person they are interacting with. People from the Mediterranean, Middle East and South America, for example, tend to touch more and require less personal space when interacting than people from Western European and Scandinavian countries. The latter generally prefer only formal touching, such as brief handshakes, and plenty of personal space unless they know the other person extremely well. We tend to require less personal space when our relationship with the other person is a close or personal one. Relationships that are more formal and less personal, such as with work colleagues, tend to demand greater physical distance for interactions to be comfortable and effective.

There are many different situations where a health and social care worker will be required to make a judgement about 'personal space'. A service user, if they are able, will usually adjust their proximity by moving their chair or standing position to acquire the amount of personal space they need during an interaction.
However, if the person is not physically able to do this, or lacks the confidence to do so, a health and social care worker who is aware of the person's discomfort and the reason for it, would be able to improve the quality of the communication by adjusting their own proximity.

Written communication

Services users' records, organisational policies and procedures, official letters and memos, e-mails and text messages between health and social care workers are all examples of written communication with care settings.

Health and social care workers spend a lot of time writing because they have to plan and document the care that they provide, evaluate their plans and write reports and referral letters about service users. Many care organisations have official record keeping systems, standard forms and report systems and employ administration staff to manage the large amount of paper work that is involved in care work. As a result, health and social care workers need to develop clear, effective writing skills and should have a good knowledge and understanding of ways of writing different kinds of document (such as patients' notes, reports and formal letters). Many of the specific writing skills needed are learnt in practice and quickly become incorporated into a care worker's practise. However, it is important for health and social care workers to regularly review and reflect on their written communication skills to ensure they are using them as effectively as possible.

See also – Communication approaches; Communication theories; Braille; British Sign Language; Makaton

Communication theories

Communication theories aim to provide theory-based explanations or accounts of the process of human communication. Health and social care workers learn about and try to apply a number of communication theories in their everyday care practice.

Argyle's stages of the communication cycle.
Michael Argyle (1925-2002) was a British social psychologist who researched and developed theories about human communication and interpersonal interaction. He focused on both verbal and non-verbal communication, carrying out experimental research to test and develop his theoretical ideas (see Argyle, 1967, 1969 and 1975). Argyle's 'communication cycle' theory sets out to understand, explain and predict how communication occurs between people in one-to-one situations.

In *The Psychology of Interpersonal Behaviour* (1967), Argyle proposed that communication is a skill that needs to be learned and practiced like any other skill. Argyle's (1967) claim was that human communication is essentially a two-way process that involves people sending, receiving and responding to each other's verbal and non-verbal 'messages'.

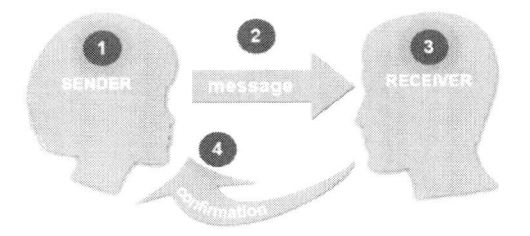

Figure 8 – The communication cycle is based on a process of sending and receiving 'messages'.

There are six main stages in the communication cycle:

1. An idea occurs
2. A 'message' is coded (by choosing words, using NVC or sign language, for example).
3. A 'message' is sent (via speech, writing, signing or use of NVC)
4. The 'message' is received
5. The 'message is decoded (the recipient has to interpret the message using their knowledge of language, NVC, signs or symbols, for example)
6. The 'message' is understood (the recipient correctly interprets the message or understands the information sent).

The receiver of a message keeps communication going by responding or giving feedback to the original 'message'. This process then repeats and builds into a communication cycle.

The concept of a 'communication cycle' makes it clear that effective communication, especially in health and social care situations, is a two-way process. As well as getting their 'messages' across to others in a clear and unambiguous way, care professionals need to understand and respond to the verbal and non-verbal feedback of the people they communicate and interact with. According to Argyle's (1967) theory, care professionals can improve the effectiveness of their communication and interaction skills by adapting to verbal and non-verbal 'feedback' from others.

Tuckman's stages of group interaction.

Care practitioners need to have an understanding of group processes and patterns of group behaviour in order to interact and communicate well in the various group situations that they experience. Understanding how groups form and then develop is an important part of this. Bruce Tuckman (1965) outlined a model of group development based around a number of stages or sequences of group activity.

Tuckman's (1965) theory suggests that groups must go through these stages to be effective and that the pattern of communication in each of the four stages or sequences is different:

- Forming is the first stage. It involves group members coming together and asking basic questions about the purpose and aims of the group, their role within it and considering whether they want to commit themselves to becoming involved in it. In this early stage of group development members tend to feel quite anxious, often prioritise their own interests and may feel 'disorientated' in their interactions with others. A leader often emerges in this early stage.
- Storming is the second stage in the group's development. As the term suggests, this is a period of conflict within the group. Members may argue over the purpose of the group, may contest its aims and sometimes resist the authority and role of the leader. This stage is one in which power and control are the main issues. Eventually the purpose of the group and roles within it becomes clearer as power and control battles are won and lost. Without tolerance and patience at this stage, the team will fail. Co-operation between members should begin to develop towards the end of this phase.
- Norming is the stage when the group's identity develops. A strong set of shared values, norms of behaviour and a group 'culture' emerges. The group manages to have one goal and

agree a shared plan to achieve it. The group becomes more cohesive and tends to work together to resolve conflicts.
- Performing is the stage when the group finally matures and gets down to working effectively. Members tend to focus more on the overall goal rather than on relationships between themselves. Relationships have by this stage become more comfortable and are based on trust and mutual support. The group now performs more effectively.

A group may or may not reach the performing stage. Effective, high performing teams do get to this stage. However, other less effective groups may get stuck at one of the earlier stages of group development if they are unable to resolve the challenges or crises associated with a particular stage of group development. Effective communication within a group situation is a key influence on whether a group reaches the performing stage.

Berne's theory of Transactional Analysis.
Eric Berne (1910-1970) was a Canadian Psychiatrist who developed a communication theory called Transactional Analysis (TA). Berne's theory was based on psychoanalytic ideas which he developed in a distinctive way. Berne (1964) suggested that people can be seen as 'actors' in their own life and 'play games' using certain 'scripts'. He wasn't suggesting that people deliberately 'act' in a false way when relating to others. What he did mean, however, was that people are not always consciously aware of why they act in the ways they do. Berne argued that people develop certain patterns of behaviour or 'scripts' that they use habitually (and unconsciously) unless they become aware of the games they are playing.

Berne suggested that interactions between people could be understood in terms of four different types of 'game' which had particular dynamics. He named these dynamics:
- 'I'm ok, you're ok' – that is, both people are content and feel that they have achieved what they wanted to.

- 'I'm ok, you're not ok' – that is, one person thinks they are superior to the other and perhaps bullies or undermines them.
- 'I'm not ok, you're ok' – that is, one person treats the other person as their rescuer or saviour. For example, in a care setting a service user may relate to a health and social care worker as an 'expert' who can make them better. This is not healthy because it is unequal and based on a power imbalance.
- 'I'm not ok, you're not ok' – that is, both people interact as if they are 'victims' in need of help and define themselves in terms of their problems. This is also unhealthy and unproductive for both participants.

Berne's transactional analysis theory also proposes that adults interact and communicate with each other using one of three 'ego states': Child; Adult; or Parent. In summary:

- when we use the child ego state we are spontaneous and playful, but also prone to moods and tantrums
- when we use the adult ego state we are balanced, can see our own and other people's strengths and weaknesses, and can accept these.
- when we use the parent ego state we are either controlling and punitive or nurturing and caring.

HEALTH AND SOCIAL CARE

Berne thought that these ego states are a feature of every adult's personality and that we always use one of them when interacting with other adults. The ego state we interact from depends on who we are interacting with and the type of situation we find ourselves in. Berne also argued that because our 'transactions' with others usually occur at an unconscious level (i.e we don't usually make a deliberate, careful choice about *how* we respond to people), we often find ourselves reacting to the role other people take. This can mean that if someone uses the Parent ego state and seems to be telling us off or disapproving about something, we sometimes find ourselves in Child mode (getting angry back, being upset and storming off, for example). Berne claimed that a mature, psychologically healthy adult ought to see what was going on and would choose to reply using their Adult ego state. This would change the 'game' from 'I'm ok, you're not okay' to an 'I'm okay, you're okay' situation.

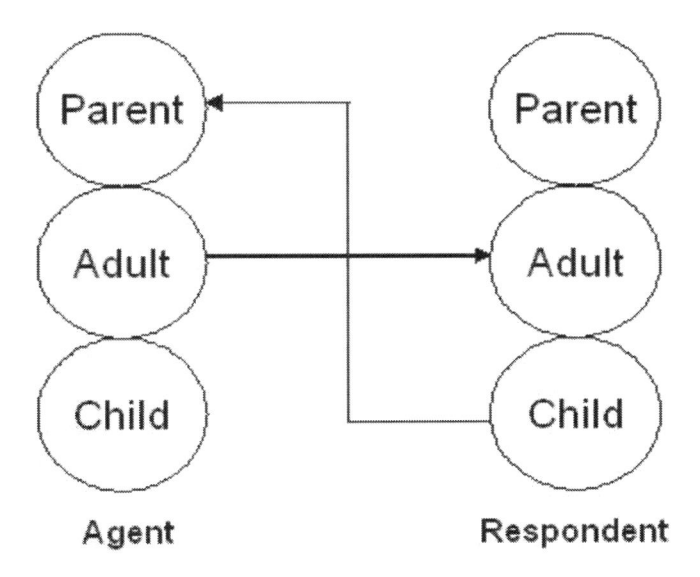

Figure 9 – Berne (1964) identified various 'games' people play using three different ego states.

Health and social care workers can use Berne's TA theory and the concepts and strategies he outlined to reflect on and understand the impact of their own communication and interaction style. Being more reflective and self-aware is always beneficial to health and social care workers as it enables them to communicate more effectively with services users and colleagues. Understanding basic TA principles can also help health and social care workers to analyse and understand the interaction patterns of service users and can be a way of helping people to avoid or reduce conflict in their relationships and achieve healthier interaction patterns.

See also – Communication approaches; Communication skills

References
Argyle, M (1967), *The Psychology of Interpersonal Behaviour*, Penguin
Argyle, M (1969), *Social Interaction*, Tavistock Publications
Argyle, M (1975), Bodily Communication, Methuen
Berne, E. (1964) *Games People Play – The Basic Hand Book of Transactional Analysis.* New York: Ballantine Books
Tuckman, B.W. (1965), 'Developmental sequences in small groups', *Psychological Bulletin*, 63, 384-99

Communication technologies

A technology is a scientific or industrial process, invention or method of doing something. Communication technologies refer to electronic / digital aids and processes that are used to help people communicate.

A range of communication technologies exist to enable people with specific communication problems – such as hearing, speech or visual impairment – to communicate with others more effectively. These include:

- **Hearing aids** containing powerful battery-powered microphones that pick up and transmit sound into the person's ear at a volume they can hear. Modern hearing aids are very small and discrete allowing a person to wear them without others really noticing. Hearing aid users may also lip-read, particularly in noisy environments where background noise is also picked up and amplified by their hearing aids, to understand what a speaker is saying to them.
- **Loop systems** are also designed to help people with hearing impairment to receive sounds that they are otherwise unable to hear. A loop is a cable that surrounds a particular area (a whole room, desk or a counter, for example). The speaker wears or uses a special microphone that amplified sound which is then picked up by a person wearing a hearing aid set to the 'loop' setting.
- **Braille** software is a form of computer-based software that creates Braille cells which are then printed out on a special braille printer. A visually impaired person can then 'read' the print out using touch.
- **Mobile phones and minicoms** can be used to send text-based messages to hearing impaired people, buzzing or vibrating to let them know a message has arrived. Obviously visually impaired

people can also use mobile phones to receive and send calls in the usual way.
- **Speech recognition software** enables visually impaired people to produce computer-based text without having to type via a keyboard. Speaking into the computer's microphone activates the software which translates what is said onto the screen.
- **Voice-activated software** is similar to speech-recognition software in that users speak to a software-based system that is typically linked to a piece of hardware, such as a specially-made wheelchair or other piece of equipment, which then turns the instructions into has been given into some form of movement or other action. This type of software is particularly useful to people with physical disabilities that impair their movement.

See also – Communication boards; Communication skills; Communication theories

HEALTH AND SOCIAL CARE

Common Assessment Framework (CAF)

The Common Assessment Framework (CAF) is a single, combined assessment process used by organisations providing children's services to identify children's additional care and support needs. CAF promotes and standardises the assessment of children's needs to ensure high quality, comprehensive services are provided in a coordinated way.

CAF provides:

- A common set of processes for practitioners to follow if they think a child would benefit.
- A common method for assessing the needs of children / young people based on models of children's development and concepts of wellbeing.
- Guidance on how to record findings and gain consent.
- Guidance on the roles and responsibilities of practitioners and agencies.

The CAF is for children who have additional needs in one or more of three areas:

1. Their growth and development.
2. Additional educational requirements.
3. Family and environmental issues and any specific needs of the child's parent or carer.

If any of these needs are identified by a practitioner, they can record the level of concern and interventions required. The CAF consists of:
- A pre-assessment checklist (to determine whether a child would benefit from a common assessment)

- A process (this enables practitioners to undertake a common assessment and then act on the result)
- A standard form (record the assessment)
- A delivery plan (and a review form)
- Standing alone (a consent statement)

The CAF approach is intended for early intervention. Assessment can take place in a universal setting (e.g a nursery, pre-school or primary school). It usually involves a multi-agency approach with appropriate information-sharing between professionals. Any professional working with a child / young person who may have additional needs should be able to carry out a good quality assessment using their organisations CAF system. This should also be inclusive of the child and their parents (where appropriate) and may lead to referral for more specialist services and assessment.

The CAF aims to move health, social care and education workers away from focusing on a child's short-term needs and their eligibility for support services towards a longer-term view of how services should, or could, be provided across the child's lifespan. The rationale for this is to focus on outcomes that can be monitored and achieved for a particular child through carefully chosen interventions and support that have an individualised, holistic focus.

As the CAF is a voluntary assessment, a child/ young person or parent/ carer must give their consent at the start of the process with full knowledge of what will happen. Once the assessment has been completed, the child and or parent / carer must also give their consent for the information to be stored and shared with other services.

See also – Confidentiality; National Eligibility Criteria; National Framework for NHS Continuing Healthcare.

Confidentiality

Confidentiality involves safeguarding the privacy of an individual's personal information.

Confidentiality is a very important care value. In practice it involves receiving, recording, storing and sharing information about people in an appropriate way. Health and social care workers have a professional and legal duty to maintain confidentiality at all times. Information must be handled carefully so that:

- an individual's wishes and privacy are respected
- the organisation's policies and procedures on confidentiality are followed
- the law is followed

Health and social care workers often obtain information when carrying out assessments or admitting people to a service for care or treatment. When doing this they should ensure that:

- they only collect information that is actually required
- the information they collect is used only for the intended purpose
- the individual's records containing the information are kept safe and secure
- all data protection guidelines are followed

Health and social care service users generally expect information about themselves to only be shared with health and social care workers who have a legitimate need to know. It should not be freely and irresponsibly shared with other third parties. However, there are some circumstances in which confidentiality can, or must, be breached. These include situations where:

- it is necessary to protect a person's health

- a person appears to be about to commit a crime
- it is necessary to protect the health or safety of others
- a court or tribunal orders certain information be disclosed
- it is necessary to help an investigation into suspected abuse.

Health and social care workers employed in all types of care settings maintain confidentiality by:

- keeping themselves informed of relevant laws relating to confidentiality
- understanding and putting into practice the professional code of conduct that they are required to follow
- knowing about and following the policies and procedures (agreed ways of working) of their employer
- ensuring that confidential information is locked away or stored on password protected computer systems
- sharing information only with people who are entitled to have access to it (the 'need to know' principle), such as multi-disciplinary team colleagues or, if consent has been given, an individual's carer or family members.

See also – Care values; Data Protection Act 1995; Health and Social Care Act 2012

Conflict / conflict management

Conflict involves disagreement, friction or discord between individuals or within a group of people. It often occurs when the beliefs or actions of one person (or one or more members of a group) are felt to be unacceptable, are rejected or are resisted by another (or other group members).

Relationships in health and social care settings and teams can sometimes generate conflict. This is common and should not necessarily be seen as a sign of bad, broken or dysfunctional relationships. Tensions arise and are sometimes expressed in conflict-based behaviour or speech in both personal and professional relationships. It isn't possible to avoid conflict or to live a conflict-free life.

Conflicts in health and social care settings may be real or imagined, temporary or permanent and result from something that has happened in the past or from a recent situation. We can sometimes anticipate when conflict is likely to occur though this is not always possible. When it does occur, there are a variety of ways of responding to conflict situations (see Figure 9).

Figure 10 – Strategies for responding to conflict

Strategy	What does this involve?	Issues to consider
Exit	'Leaving' the relationship physically or mentally	Does the person have a choice to leave the relationship? Are people supported in articulating their wish to end the relationship?
Voice	Discussing the issues	Can the person complain or express dissatisfaction? Is the person's view taken seriously? Will changes be made?
Loyalty	Waiting / hoping for improvements in the relationship	Is the person able to establish an 'exit' point or is this situation ongoing?
Neglect	Allowing the relationship to gradually dissolve / making no effort to address issues.	Does neglect happen because support to maintain the relationship is missing?

A person's ability to respond appropriately to conflict will be influenced by their:

- relationship with that person
- self-worth, self-esteem and self-confidence

HEALTH AND SOCIAL CARE

Health and social care workers experience conflict from a number of sources. Patients / service users, their families and friends, colleagues and other organisational staff, people working for other agencies and media organisations often have comments to make about the way care services are being (or are not being) provided.

Some patients and their family members may feel upset about the way they have been – or haven't been – treated, about the quality of care facilities, about waiting times or about the cost or outcomes of their care, for example. Dissatisfaction and complaints can be difficult to manage when people are upset, frightened or in shock because of unexpected health problems or have been given bad news.

Frontline health and social care workers are often the first people to face these complaints and the strong emotions that some people express. As a result, it is important to know:

- how to handle and de-escalate conflict
- how to respond constructively to conflict and complaints
- what an organisation's complaints policy and procedures say
- how to support patients and service users to use the complaints procedure
- how to use supervision to talk about and get support to deal with the personal impact that episodes of conflict can have.

Effective communication skills, the use of active listening and empathy and a commitment to putting care values into practice can all help to minimise and address conflict when it occurs in health and social care settings.

See also – Communication skills

Consequentialism

Consequentialism is a philosophical approach, or way of thinking about, ethics. As its name implies, consequentialism is concerned with the outcomes or consequences of a particular course of action or decision. Jeremy Bentham (1794 – 1832) and John Stuart Mill (1806 – 1873) are the philosophers most closely associated with consequentialism.

Health and social care workers, and medical practitioners in particular, sometimes have to make decisions or decide what to do in situations that are ethically difficult. How can they do this? The consequentialist approach encourages people in this situation to focus on achieving an ethically acceptable outcome, one that leads to the best result for an individual's health or wellbeing or that of others affected by the decision. But who decides what the 'best' result it?

In practice, using a consequentialist approach can result in a person's wishes or 'autonomy' being over-ridden on the grounds that it is in their own interest, or will promote a greater public good, to do so. For example, from a consequentialist position, it would be ethically justifiable to admit a person to hospital involuntarily (against their will) in order to protect them or others from harm or distress even though this goes against the principles of autonomy and respect.

HEALTH AND SOCIAL CARE

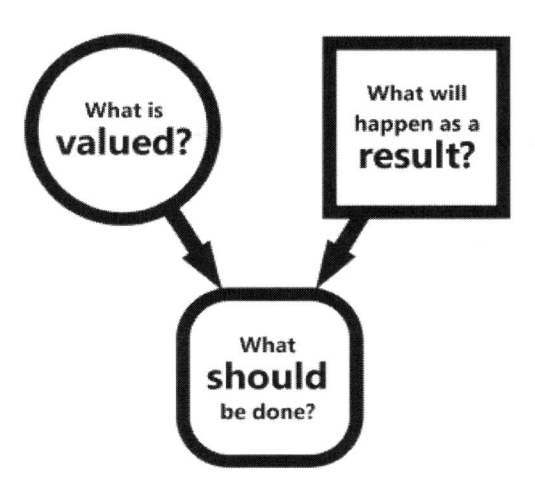

Figure 11 – These are the kinds of questions a consequentialist would ask.

> ***See also*** – Autonomy; Care value base; Deontology; Ethical issues; Principlism;

Data Protection Act 1998

This Act established clear requirements about access to 'personal data', how a service user can ask to see their records and how long it should take staff to prepare the records before they can be seen. Data users, such as NHS Trusts and local authority social services departments, are required to register their recording and use of service users' personal data with the Data Protection Registrar. They must then comply with the following Data Protection Act principles:

Personal data must:

- Be collected and processed fairly and lawfully
- Only be held for specific, lawful registered purposes
- Only be used for registered purposes or disclosed to registered recipients
- Be adequate and relevant to the purpose for which it is held;
- Be accurate and, where necessary, kept up to date
- Be held no longer than is necessary for the state purpose
- Be surrounded by appropriate security
- Be subject to a right of access by the data subject (to records held about himself)

Service users are entitled to know whether any information about them is being held by a care organisation. If it is they have the right to apply to see and be given access to a copy of it. Access to health records can be denied where the disclosure of the contents:

- would be likely to cause serious harm to the physical or mental health of the data subject
- would reveal the identity of others (not including care professionals) who have provided information in confidence and

HEALTH AND SOCIAL CARE

who have not then consented to it or their identity being disclosed.

Permission to see personal health records has to be sought from and given by the medical practitioner who is responsible for the service user's care. Applications must be made in writing and are also subject to the payment of a fee. Unless the exception principles given above apply, the applicant is entitled to a copy of the information contained in their records within 40 days of application. If this is not forthcoming they can go to Court to enforce their legal right or obtain enforcement from the Data Protection Registrar.

Figure 12 – The Data Protection Act 1998 provides a legal framework for protecting sensitive data.

See also – Confidentiality; Freedom of Information Act 2000; HCPC (codes of practice); Health and Social Care Act 2012.

Deontology

Deontology is an approach to ethics and ethical theory that focuses on moral duty and the 'rightness' (in moral terms) of the actions people take through their behaviour or decision-making. *Deon* is a Greek term for *obligation* or *duty*.

Immanuel Kant (1742 – 1804), a German philosopher, epitomised the deontological approach when he stated 'Let justice be done even if the heaves fall'. What he meant was that a person should always make a decision that they believe is morally right, regardless of the consequences. This last bit is quite important and is one of the reasons why critics of deontology argue that it isn't quite so ethical after all. What if a decision leads, or is likely to lead, to negative or unfortunate consequences? Deontologists say the decision should – or perhaps must – be made if it is morally justifiable, regardless of unwanted or negative outcomes.

Essentially deontologists try to promote human freedom and rationality. For example, a health and social care worker who had to decide whether to admit somebody to a mental health unit against their will would probably prioritise the individual's right to 'respect' and 'autonomy'. This may seem like a positive, empowering approach to take but it is important to note that apparently 'ethical' decisions like this can also result in bad outcomes. What if the person's wish for autonomy is respected but then they harm themselves or other people? This would probably concern a lot of health and social care workers. However, from a deontological perspective what is important is how a decision is reached not what its consequences might be.

See also – Autonomy; Consequentialism; Care values; Deontology; Principlism; Virtue ethics.

Discrimination

The term discrimination can be used in a number of ways. For example, discrimination involves recognizing and understanding the difference between one thing and another, such as when we discriminate between right and wrong or good and bad. This isn't the way in which health and social care workers tend to use or understand this term. This is because discrimination – or more precisely unfair discrimination – also refers to the unjust and unfair treatment of different categories of people because of their race, age, gender or sexuality, for example.

Figure 13 – Discrimination is an important issue that affects many people who use and provide health and social care services.

Unfair discrimination can be expressed and experienced in a number of different ways:

- **Direct discrimination** involves deliberately treating one person less favourably than another and can be an overt abuse of power. The motive or intention behind such treatment is irrelevant. For example, unlawful direct discrimination would occur if a residential home refused to admit a disabled black person as a resident simply because she was black. It is also unlawful for residential homes to set quotas admitting people of different ethnic origins or to reserve places on a racial basis as this would lead to direct discrimination.

- **Indirect discrimination**, or the covert use of power, can also occur, for example, where a residential home sets a requirement or condition that when applied equally disadvantages some social groups because they are less able to satisfy it. Because the condition or requirement works to the detriment of some social groups (and to the advantage of others) it indirectly discriminates against them.

Unfair discrimination doesn't just occur at an individual, interpersonal level. Institutions, including care organisations, have also been accused of operating in ways that discriminate unfairly. Institutional discrimination is usually associated with indirect forms of discrimination. This can occur, for example, where the policies or procedures of a care organisation disadvantage a particular social group whose members are less able to comply with it.

Unfair discrimination that is obvious and deliberate is known as overt discrimination. Unfair discrimination that happens inadvertently or which is carried out in a secretive, hidden way is known as covert discrimination. Acknowledging diversity and challenging prejudices and all forms of unfair discrimination are important elements of anti-discriminatory practice in care work.

HEALTH AND SOCIAL CARE

Figure 14 – Examples of unfair discrimination

Type of discrimination	What does this involve?
Racism	Unfair discrimination against people because of their 'race' or ethnicity. It can be expressed as: • institutional racism where an organisation inadvertently disadvantages or deliberately treats people of one particular ethnic group less favourably • directly as overt racism • indirectly as covert or inadvertent racism Minority ethnic groups are more likely to experience racism than members of the White majority group in the UK.
Sexism	Unfair discrimination against people because of their sex or gender. Sexism: • can occur at institutional, group or an individual level • may be direct and overt r indirect, inadvertent and covert Women are more likely to experience sexism in the UK. The consequences can be fewer opportunities, lack of recognition and unequal pay compared to men, for example.
Homophobia	This is the fear and hatred of people who are homosexual and their homosexuality. Homophobia is a prejudice that can lead to: • hostility and unfair discrimination • hate crimes • physical threats and violence People who are homophobic often feel that heterosexuality is 'normal' and that homosexuality somehow presents a threat to normal social order.

See also – Anti-discriminatory practice; Diversity; Equality

Diversity

Diversity refers to the social, cultural or ethnic differences in the characteristics of individuals within a population.

Diversity is a feature of modern life. The United Kingdom has a population that is diverse in many ways. That is, the population consists of people who have a range of different characteristics, needs, beliefs and values. Diversity within the UK population can be understood in terms of:

- 'race' / ethnicity
- culture
- gender
- social class
- sexuality
- disability
- age

All of these social and cultural differences affect people's needs and have important implications for care practitioners and for care organisations. In particular, health and social care practice needs to acknowledge, respect and accommodate this diversity. Care organisations and practitioners have to meet the particular needs of people of different ages, different genders, people who have differing ethnic and cultural backgrounds and people with a broad range of abilities, disabilities, illnesses and impairments whilst also ensuring people are treated equally. Health and social care workers need to understand the benefits of social and cultural diversity in order to provide appropriate care services in a fair and equal way.

HEALTH AND SOCIAL CARE

Diversity is not celebrated by everyone in the UK and is a source of fear and resentment for some people who believe they are being 'pushed out' or 'taken over' by 'outsiders'. This can then lead to unfair treatment or unfair discrimination against those who are different from the majority.

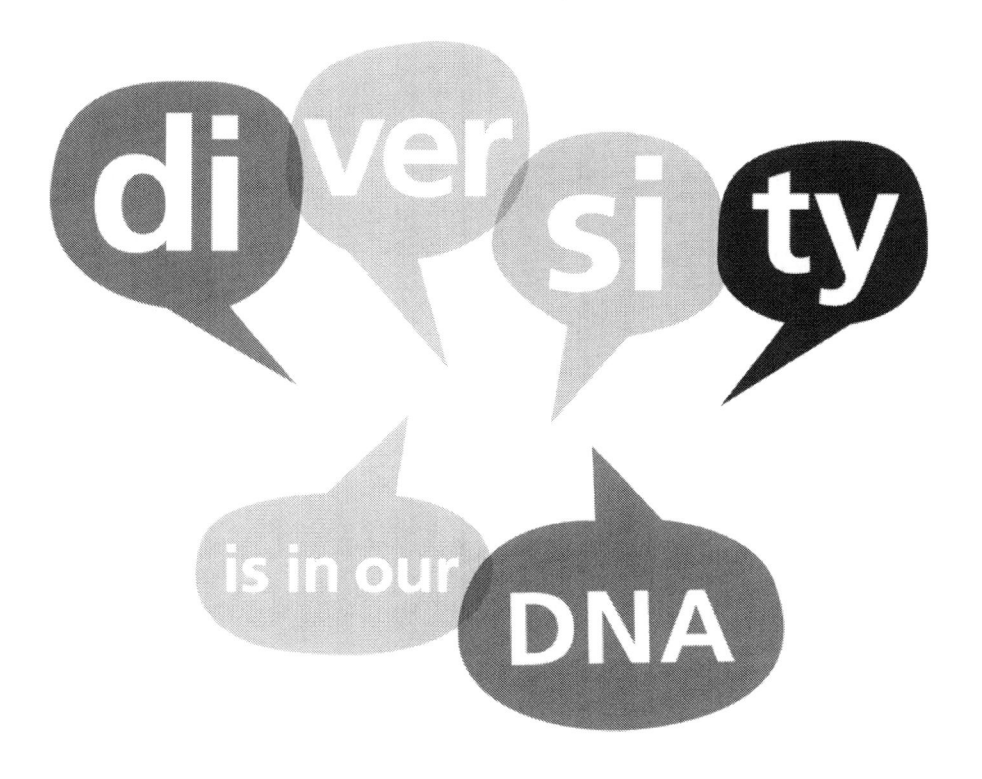

Figure 15 – Diversity is an important issue for everyone in health and social care settings.

See also – Advocacy; Anti-discriminatory practice; Discrimination; Equality;

Education, Health and Care plan

Education, Health and Care Plans (EHPs) were introduced across England and Wales in 2014. EHPs have replaced the previous system of Individual Healthcare Plans (IHPs) that were developed for children and young people with special educational needs (SEN).

EHPs were developed to help address the support needs of children and young people under 25 who have complex and multiple needs that span health, social care and education services. Their purpose is to ensure that a full holistic needs assessment is carried out to identify and then coordinate individualised assistance, care and support for a child. The EHC will focus on these needs and also the individual requirements and personality of the child.

An example of a brief EHC Plan,
A child suffering from type 1 diabetes will need to monitor their blood sugar levels at least once during the school day. This will usually be done during the mid-day lunch break. Should the child report a low reading, the staff member should provide the child with a sugary food and drink. Similarly, with insulin injections, the child may need to be excused from class when feeling light-headed or drowsy in order to restore their levels to a safe state.

The draft EHP should be shared between the parent(s), education workers and any personal assistants the child has. Once agreed, the Headteacher is responsible for informing all staff about a child's care and support needs and ensuring staff members can implement the EHC and respond to emergency situations. EHCs should be shared and reviewed annually.

See also – Common Assessment Process (CAF); Education professionals; Healthcare commissioning.

Education professionals

Education professionals are teachers, administrators, support staff and specialists such as educational psychologists employed within education services.

Education professionals work with infants, children, adolescents and adults of all ages and abilities. They may be employed in mainstream early years / pre-school (under 5), infant, primary or secondary school settings as well as in sixth form and further education colleges and universities. In addition, education professionals are also employed in a range of specialist settings that overlap with, or have strong links to, health and social care provision. These may include, for example, SureStart / early years centres, hospital-based schools, special schools for children with learning disabilities or behavioural difficulties, tuition centres for children excluded from school, secure units for children and adolescents, mental health units and community centres.

Health and social care practitioners may work with education professionals as part of a multi-agency / multi-disciplinary team in a setting where service users (children, adolescents or adults) have a range of developmental, educational and care or support needs. An example of this would be a Child and Adolescent Mental Health team (CAMHS) where both educational and mental health or behavioural support services need to be provided for service users. Health and social care workers and educational professionals would need to collaborate on and share assessment information to establish each child's needs, plan their support or interventions and would also need to liaise regularly to monitor and share information about a child's progress and/or response to planned interventions.

See also – Education, Health and Care Plan; Healthcare professionals; Multi-agency working; Multi-disciplinary team; Social care professionals.

Empathy

Empathy involves a person putting themselves in another person's position to appreciate how they feel or what they think about something.

How would you like it if the mouse did that to you?

The concept of empathy originates from humanistic psychology. This has a focus on the self and on developing an holistic understanding that acknowledges and accepts the individual's thoughts, feelings and experiences as being an important part of who they are.

Being empathic is often quite difficult to do and is distinct from sympathy. The listener needs to put aside any preconceptions they have in order to recognise how the person is struggling to deal with specific problems. They need to be able to 'tune in' to the person's feelings and to use their own emotions intelligently to experience empathy. Empathy does not involve making any guesses or assumptions about what the other person is *really* thinking or feeling. Tschudin (1982) uses the metaphor of helping a man stuck in a ditch to illustrate the difference between empathy and sympathy:

"The sympathetic helper goes and lies in the ditch with him and bewails the situation with him. The unsympathetic helper stands on the bank and shouts 'come on, get yourself out of that ditch!' The empathic helper climbs down to the victim but keeps one foot on the bank and is thus able to help the victim out of the trouble on to firm ground again."

Empathy is an important skill that can be used by health and social care workers in many different situations. It is particularly relevant to situations where a person's emotional wellbeing is fragile or a concern. Health and social care workers can make their interactions with service users, family members and colleagues more effective by using empathy appropriately, gaining insight into the needs and experience of service users in an alert, calm way, without having to actually experience it directly. Using empathy also gives health and social care workers a way of communicating with the real person behind the label of service user, relative or colleague.

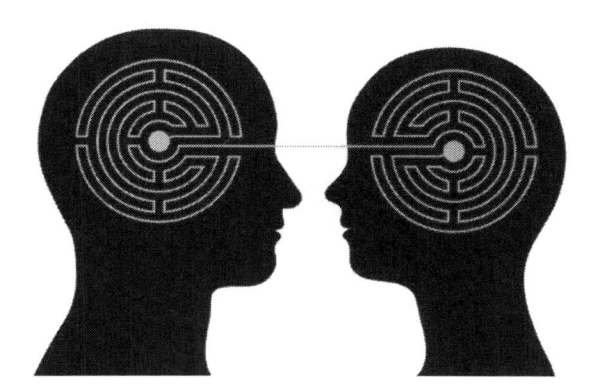

Figure 16 – Empathy involves awareness of another person's feelings and point of view.

See also – Attachment; Care values; Communication approaches;
References
V. Tschudin (1982) *Counselling skills for Nurses*, Bailliere Tindall.

Ethical issues

One way of explaining 'ethics' is to see them as principles linked to a fundamental sense of 'right' and 'wrong', 'good' and 'bad'. From this perspective, we all have a set of 'ethics' that guide our behaviour. The ethics we abide by provide us all with a set of moral norms or benchmarks that influence our standards of personal and professional behaviour.

Figure 17 - 'What should I (or we) do?' is an important ethical issue often faced by health and social care workers.

Health and social care practitioners are often faced with sensitive and difficult situations in which they have to make a decision. These could include, for example:

- Should I refer this person for an investigative scan or 'wait and see' whether further symptoms develop?

- Should this person be detained against their will in a mental health unit?
- Is it time to stop giving this person potentially life-saving CPR as they don't seem to be responding or should we carry on in the hope that they will?
- Should we keep this person on a life-support machine or should we switch it off?

In situations like these, there is often no obvious or clearly correct answer. Health and social care practitioners face ethical dilemmas when they have to work out what the 'right' (ethical) course of action is.

As well as providing guidance on how to behave (such as to 'protect confidentiality' or 'accept diversity'), the ethics and care values that health and social care workers draw on point them towards morally acceptable ways of behaving and relating to others.

Ethical principles and care values tell us how we *ought* to behave and provide us with benchmarks or norms against which to assess our own and other peoples' attitudes, decisions and behaviour. They are vital in helping health and social care workers deal with the frequent ethical dilemmas they face.

See also – Care values; Conflict; Confidentiality; Consequentialism; Deontology; Principlism; Risk; Virtue ethics

Equality

In health and social care contexts, equality involves treating everyone who uses care services (or who works within them) in a fair and equal way.

Equality is a wide-ranging term with a number of different meanings. Where people expect to receive equal or fair <u>access</u> to treatment or services they are referring to *equality of opportunity* or *equal rights*. The slightly different idea that people are entitled to an equal <u>share</u> of health and social care resources (e.g a practitioner's time or a particular drug treatment) is summed up by the concept of *equity*. Where treatment is provided equitably, every service user will receive their fair share of resources.

The various forms of social inequality that exist in British society can lead some people to experience social exclusion and the negative health effects of social disadvantage, prejudice and unfair discrimination. These effects can be seen in the higher rates of illness, disease and premature death that people in the lower social classes and those in marginalised groups experience. It is important to note that social inequality is not a consequence of the physical, social or cultural differences that exist in the population. It is the unequal distribution of economic and social resources, prejudice and unfair discrimination and the inability, or reluctance, of governments, organisations and individuals to tackle sources of privilege and social advantage that have the effect of creating and maintaining social inequalities.

See also – Advocacy; Anti-discriminatory practice; Discrimination; Diversity;

HEALTH AND SOCIAL CARE

Freedom of Information Act 2000

The purpose of the Freedom of Information Act 2000 is to give members of the public access to information held by public authorities in England, Wales and Northern Ireland as well as any UK-wide authorities that are based in Scotland. Public authorities include government departments, local authorities, the NHS, state schools and police forces. Charities and private sector organisations are not covered by The FOI Act 2000.

Freedom of Information Act 2000

Figure 18 – The Freedom of Information Act 2000 applies to all NHS and local authority service providers.

Under the Freedom of Information Act 2000, public authorities have:
- to publish certain information about their activities.
- a duty to respond to members of the public who request certain information from them.

There is a presumption of disclosure under the FOI Act 2000. This means that a public authority has to provide the requested information unless it can give a valid and justifiable reason for not doing so. The person requesting the information does not have to give a reason for, or justify, their request.

The FOI Act 2000 does not give an individual access to information about themselves that is held by public authorities. This can be done using the provision of the Data Protection Act 1998. The FOI Act 2000 enables interested parties, including individuals and organisations, to hold public authorities to account by requiring them to divulge information that may be relevant to decisions, developments or practices that may affect an individual, group or community. This often happens when local or national media organisations request information about staffing levels, bed occupancy levels and the budgets or spending patterns of NHS Trusts or other providers of health and social care services.

The argument in favour of obtaining this kind of information is that it allows more informed public debate to occur and also makes public authorities – who should be working in the public interest – to be held more accountable for their decisions and actions.

See also – Confidentiality; Legislation.

Health Action Plans

Health Action Plans (HAP) are structured, focused documents that are designed to support young people and adults with learning disabilities to think about ways of being healthy and about getting the healthcare support and services they may need.

Health Action Plans have been developed by the Department for Health as part of the *Valuing People* (2001) strategy that aims to improve the physical and mental health and wellbeing of learning disabled people. The plans are designed to be inclusive and shared so that the individual contributes to and retains a copy of their HAP in an easy-to-read, accessible format whilst their GP and any other healthcare providers involved with them also retains a copy in a written, word-based and often digital format. The Department of Health leaflet written for learning disabled people explains the HAP in the following terms:

Your Health Action Plan will have information about things you can do to be healthy, like:

- *Getting the right information about your health*
- *Doing the right things to look after yourself if you have problems with your health*
- *Talking to a doctor or nurse if you are ill, worried about your health, or in hospital*
- *Talking to other people who can help you keep healthy*
- *Eating food that is good for you*
- *Doing exercise*
- *Being safe at home, or when you are out*
- *Getting your eyes, ears and teeth checked*
- *Having enough money and somewhere nice to live*
- *Having friends and interesting things to do.*

Health Action Plans aim to promote personalised care and support for all people with learning disabilities, who would otherwise struggle to have their individual needs recognised within health care services.

> ***See also*** – Common Assessment Framework (CAF); Individual needs; Personalised care.
>
> **References**
> Department for Health (2001) *Valuing People*, DOH

Health and Care Professions Council (HCPC) codes of practice

The Health and Care Professions Council is a regulatory body that maintains the professional registers for a variety of health and social care professions. These include social workers, occupational therapists, physiotherapists, podiatrists, dieticians, paramedics and radiographers, for example.

The HCPC produce a number of codes of practice to regulate the practice (i.e the behaviour and conduct) of the professionals on their Register. With regard to managing information, the HCPC standards of conduct, performance and ethics tell registrants:

> **You must respect the confidentiality of service users.**
> You must treat information about service users as confidential and use it only for the purposes they have provided it for. You must not knowingly release any personal or confidential information to anyone who is not entitled to it, and you should check that people who ask for information are entitled to it.
>
> You must only use information about a service user:
> – to continue to care for that person; or
> – for purposes where that person has given you permission to use the information or the law allows you to do so.
> You must also keep to the conditions of any relevant data-protection laws and always follow best practice for handling confidential information. Best practice is likely to change over time, and you must stay up to date.

Breaching confidentiality inappropriately or failing to manage information is a disciplinary offence that can (and does) lead to registered health care professionals being 'struck off' or removed from the professional register.

See also – Allied Health Professionals; Confidentiality.

Health and Social Care Act 2012

The Health and Social Care Act 2012 is an Act of Parliament or statute that is best known for changing the way the National Health Service in England is structured and organised.

The main effects of the Health and Social Care Act 2012 include:

- Removing responsibility for the health of UK citizens from the Secretary of State for Health
- Abolishing NHS primary care trusts (PCTs) and Strategic Health Authorities (SHAs)
- Establishing clinical commissioning groups – often run by GPs – to commission healthcare for local populations and manage the commissioning budgets

The Act was controversial at the time with critics claiming that the re-organisation was intended to open up opportunities for private providers of healthcare services to bid for and take over NHS provision.

Impact on information management issues
The Health and Social Care Act 2012 imposed a duty of the Care Quality Commission to develop and apply a code of practice on the management of confidential personal information. It defines 'confidential personal information' as 'information that is obtained by the Commission in terms or circumstances requiring it to be held in confidence and relates to and identifies an individual".

HEALTH AND SOCIAL CARE

Confidential personal information is likely to include (but is not limited to) information about a person's:

- Physical or mental health
- Social or family circumstances
- Financial standing and financial details
- Education, training and employment experience
- Religious beliefs
- Racial or ethnic origin
- Sexuality
- Criminal convictions

The information may relate to people who use services, their families, carers or representatives, registered providers, health and social care staff, CQC staff, or any other person who has contact with CQC. Although CQC acknowledges that some information is more sensitive than others (for example, information about a person's sexual health is more likely to be sensitive than information about a broken leg, as disclosure of that information is more likely to cause damage or distress to the person to whom it relates), they are required to apply the same principles and standards of care to all confidential personal information that they hold.

It is a criminal offence under the Health and Social Care Act 2008 for anyone to disclose confidential personal information that has been obtained by CQC, other than in certain circumstances.

See also – Confidentiality; Legislation.

Health and Social Care Information Centre (HSCIC)

Since 1 August 2016, the Health and Social Care Information Centre (HSCIC) has been known as *NHS Digital*. It part of the Department of Health, the section of government responsible for health and social care service policy and provision.

The main purpose of NHS Digital (formerly HSCIC) is to store and analyse data on hospital activity in England and to use this to produce comparative statistics on NHS activity. In particular, it analyses and produces statistics from the long-running Hospital Episode statistics. The data it produces can be used by local providers (commissioners, analysts and clinicians) to improve the quality and efficiency of frontline care provision in England.

Figure 19 – NHS Digital is the new name of the Health and Social Care Information Centre.

See also – Confidentiality.

Healthcare commissioning

Healthcare commissioning involves the identification of healthcare needs within a local population or geographical area followed by the making arrangements for the required services to be provided. A number of organisations are responsible for commissioning healthcare services in the UK. These include:

- Clinical Commissioning Groups (in England)
- Local Health Boards (in Wales)
- Health and Social Care Boards (in Northern Ireland)

Clinical Commissioning Groups (CCGs)
Clinical commissioning groups were set up by the Health and Social Care Act (2012) to organise the delivery of health care in England. CCGs are led by clinicians, mainly GPs but also other nurses and healthcare practitioners, who work in a particular geographical area. The aim is to give local practitioners influence over service commissioning decisions for their patients. CCGs are responsible for commissioning:

- elective hospital care
- rehabilitative care
- urgent / emergency care
- community health care
- mental health and learning disability services.

CCGs are overseen by NHS England. Some CCGs now commission primary health care services or have 'joint commissioning' arrangements with NHS England to do so.

Local Health Boards
Local Health Boards commission healthcare services in Wales. There are 7 Health Boards working with 3 NHS Trusts. They commission primary, hospital and community health services and provide information about health care to people locally.

Health and Social Care Boards
Health and Social Care Boards commission health care services in Northern Ireland. There are 5 Local Commissioning Groups and 5 Health and Social Care Trusts. They work together to reform and modernise healthcare services. Unusually, by comparison to England and Wales, Health and Social Care Boards commission integrated services rather than healthcare services alone.

Figure 20 – A summary of the role of clinical commissioning groups in England.

See also – Agencies; Healthcare professionals; Social care commissioning.

Healthcare professionals

A healthcare professional – or healthcare provider – is a practitioner who provides care services that have one or more of the following aims:

- promoting physical and mental health,
- preventing physical and/or mental health problems from developing,
- treating and ideally curing conditions affecting and individual's health,
- rehabilitating or re-enabling an individual who has experienced physical or mental health problems.

The term healthcare professionals is generally used to refer to registered or qualified healthcare practitioners though there are a wide range and a large number of healthcare workers who have support or assistant-type work roles too. Health care professionals can be categorised in occupational groups such as:

- allied health professionals (occupational therapists, physiotherapists, speech and language therapists, pharmacists, radiographers, operating department practitioners, etc)
- medical practitioners (doctors, surgeons, dentists)
- nursing and midwifery practitioners (adult general, children's, learning disability and mental health nurses and midwives)
- public health practitioners (e.g Health Visitors, Public Health specialists)

Health professionals require formal training and qualifications and must be registered with their professional body in order to practice. Professional bodies include the General Medical Council (Doctors), the Nursing and Midwifery Council (Nurses and Midwives) and the Health and Care Professions Council (Allied health professionals. In addition to categorising healthcare professionals by occupational group (as above), another way of doing so is to categorise them according to the area of health care provision in which they practice – such as emergency medical care, mental health care, rehabilitation, childbirth / maternity or surgical care, for example.

A healthcare professional may work in a number of different settings (in-patient, hospital-based or outpatient, community-based) and in a number of different specialist areas of their main area of practice during their career. Some healthcare professionals also move into management, research, teaching and other specialist but indirect care roles during their career.

Figure 21 – Healthcare professionals may take on a number of different roles during their careers.

See also – Allied health professionals; Multi-agency working; Multi-disciplinary teams; Social care professionals; Voluntary sector workers.

Individual needs

A need is the gap between what currently exists or is available and what a person requires or could benefit from to support or sustain their personal health and/or wellbeing.

'Need' is a key concept in health and social care practice. However, there is no overall or general agreement on what the concept of need means. As a result, it is sometimes described as a 'contested concept'. Despite this, it is a term and idea that health and social care workers use widely. Typically, it is used as shorthand for the things that an individual requires to enable them to achieve, maintain or restore their health and acceptable levels of social independence or quality of life. But who defines what is 'acceptable' or 'desirable'? No two individuals are identical and people tend to perceive and define their needs in personal ways.
Bradshaw (1972) identified four types of individual need. He called these:

- Normative need – that is, needs which are defined by professionals. They are based on normal levels or values measured against a set of standards such as percentile charts, BMI or BP.
- Felt need – this refers to the individual's perception of what they want or require. This is shaped by their experience and also depends on the person having insight into their own problems.
- Expressed needs – that is, what people say they need. This is usually reflected in a person's understanding, expectations and use of services.
- Comparative need – that is, the extent to which an individual or group has or lacks resources compared to others.

Health and social care workers are likely to come across and use these different ways of thinking about 'need' at some point in their careers. In everyday practice, care workers tend to have a less philosophical and more practical approach to identifying and meeting the individual needs of the people they care for and support. In particular, they may use one or more of the following acronyms to identify and assess an individual's needs:

- PIES – Physical, Intellectual, Emotional and Social needs
- PISCES – Physical, Intellectual, Social, Cultural, Emotional and Spiritual needs
- PROCCLESS – Physical, Relationship, Organisational, Communication, Cognitive, Cultural, Emotional, Social, Spiritual needs

Maslow's hierarchy of needs

Maslow's hierarchy of needs also provides a typology of need that is well known to and widely used by health and social care workers. Maslow's humanistic approach to development and behaviour is based on the belief that human beings have a number of different types of 'need' and that these needs must be met or satisfied in a particular sequence before the person can develop further. Specifically, a person's basic physiological needs must be met first before they can satisfy their safety and security needs. Their behaviour will then be motivated by a desire to satisfy their love and emotional needs. When these are satisfied, the person will be motivated to meet their self-esteem needs. At this point, the individual is in a position to focus on achieving their full potential or need for self-actualisation.

Maslow's concept of a hierarchy of needs has been a major influence on health and social care workers since the mid-twentieth century.

HEALTH AND SOCIAL CARE

The belief that an individual's basic physiological and safety needs must be prioritized in the way that care is provided remains central in medical and nursing practice.

Similarly, health and social care workers supporting people with non-physical social and emotional problems often draw on Maslow's insights to create support and treatment plans based on the idea that people are motivated to behave, develop and change in a needs-based way.

Self-actualisation
(Achieving individual potential)

Esteem
(self-esteem and esteem from others)

Belonging
(Love, affection, being a part of groups)

Safety
(Shelter, removal from danger)

Physiological
(Health, food, sleep)

Figure 22 - Maslow's Hierarchy of Needs

Health and social care workers require a good understanding of individual needs in order to carry out needs assessments and to use the information they obtain to develop appropriate care and treatment plans. It is important to find out about and take account of a person's felt and expressed needs whilst also applying a clinical or professional understanding of human health and wellbeing needs.

See also – Autonomy; Personalised care; Personalisation
References
Bradshaw, J. (1972) *The concept of social need*, New Society, 30 March.

Integrated Health and Social Care organisations

The World Health Organisation defines integrated care as

> "a concept bringing together inputs, delivery, management and organization of services related to diagnosis, treatment, care, rehabilitation and health promotion. Integration is a means to improve services in relation to access, quality, user satisfaction and efficiency."

Health and social care services have historically been provided by separate organisations employing staff to perform distinctive healthcare and social care roles. However, this system of parallel health and social care service provision has become increasingly outdated and difficult to sustain. Problems have included:

- the overlap or repetition of services
- lack of communication between agencies leading to failures to provide care and safeguarding
- the costs of staffing and running a parallel system
- excessive bureaucracy as separate systems and processes generate twice as much administration and paperwork as a single integrated system.

The current response to the difficulties and drawbacks of parallel health and social care systems is to develop integrated health and social care organisations. These bring together health and social care provision in an effort to provide more coordinated and integrated forms of care and support. The goal of integrating health and social care provision is that it enables agencies to respond to an individual's complex needs with a range of support, care and interventions that can be offered in a seamless, coordinated way.

HEALTH AND SOCIAL CARE

Increasingly, health and social care organisations are merging their service provision into Health and Social Care Trusts (e.g Manchester Mental Health and Social Care Trust).

> *See also* – Healthcare commissioning organisations; Social care commissioning organisations;
>
> **References**
> Gröne, O & Garcia-Barbero, M (2002): Trends in Integrated Care – Reflections on Conceptual Issues. World Health Organization, Copenhagen, 2002, EUR/02/5037864

Legislation

Legislation is the term used to describe written laws, also known as statutes and Acts of Parliament, that have been passed by Parliament in the United Kingdom.

Health, social care and early years workers in the United Kingdom are required to work within a legal and ethical framework. This means that care workers must follow and put into practice a range of laws, policies and codes of practice in their work with service users. Acts of Parliament set down the basic principles of law on particular issues, such as equality issues, in a precise and formal way. These legal principles are gradually tested and clarified when people bring cases of alleged unfair discrimination, for example, before the courts. Judges then have to look at the facts of individual cases and decide whether and how the legal principles of the Act of Parliament can be applied. When a judge makes a decision that establishes a new legal principle, perhaps because a new situation or set of circumstances has arisen, they establish a precedent. This precedent or decision then applies to all cases in which the facts are the same as (or substantially similar to) those of the original case. The series of precedents that have been established are collectively known as case law.

HEALTH AND SOCIAL CARE

Care organisations and individual health and social care workers have to abide by and incorporate into their work the various pieces of legislation that specifically apply to the care sector (e.g the Care Act 2014, Mental Health Act 2007) as well as all of the laws (e.g Equality Act 2010, Human Rights Act 1998) that affect people generally. They do this in a variety of ways. For example, care organisations produce policies and charters that set out how they intend to offer their services and conduct their business. Health and social care workers then have to ensure they put the policies into practice in their work.

See also – Data Protection Act 1998; Mental Capacity Act 2005; Mental Health Act 1998 / 2007.

Makaton

Makaton is a language system that is designed to enable individuals who can't speak to communicate with others. Makaton tends to be used by people who have cognitive impairments (e.g from brain injuries), autism, Down's syndrome or other neurological conditions that affect their ability to communicate effectively using speech.

The name 'Makaton' is derived from the initial letters of the names of three speech and language therapists who developed the system in the 1970s: Margaret Walker; Katherine Johnston; and Tony Cornforth. All worked for the Royal Association for Deaf People at the time.

As a communication system, Makaton uses a combination of speech, signs and graphic symbols. It has a core vocabulary of approximately 450 concepts that are taught and learnt in a specific order. Stage 1, for example, involves learning vocabulary for meeting an individual's immediate needs – such as 'eat' and 'drink'. At a later stage, a Makaton user will learn more complex and abstract vocabulary related to concepts such as time and emotions, for example. The core vocabulary can be learnt in a way that best suits an individual's needs and can be adapted according to the country it is being used in by supplementing it with culturally relevant signs and symbols. In the UK, Makaton users incorporate British Sign Language (BSL) signs that are mainly from the London and South East England dialect.

See also – British Sign Language; Communication boards; Communication skills.

Mental Capacity Act 2005

The Mental Capacity Act 2005 provides a range of legal protections to people who are unable to make decisions about their own life because of their mental capacity problems. 'Capacity' refers to the ability or power to do something – in this case the cognitive or mental abilities needed to process and understand information.

The Act supports each individual's right to make decisions but ensures that appropriate support is provided for people who lack mental capacity. People in this situation tend to have diagnosed mental health problems, a dementia-based condition, an intellectual (learning) disability or a neurological / brain-based disorder. As a result, the Act requires health and social care professionals to consider a person's mental capacity and to ensure five principles outlined in Section 1 of the 2005 Act are followed. These state that:

1. A person must be assumed to have capacity unless it is established that he/she lacks capacity.
2. A person is not to be treated as unable to make a decision unless all practicable steps to help him/her to do so have been taken without success.
3. A person is not to be treated as unable to make a decision merely because he/she makes an unwise decision.
4. An act done, or decision made, under this Act for or on behalf of a person who lacks capacity must be done, or made, in his/her best interests.
5. Before the act is done, or the decision is made, regard must be had to whether the purpose for which it is needed can be as effectively achieved in a way that is less restrictive of the person's rights and freedom of action.

ABC GUIDE MEETING INDIVIDUAL CARE AND SUPPORT NEEDS

The 2005 Act also introduced 'Advanced decisions' (also known as 'Living Wills') to allow people to plan ahead for a time when they may lack capacity but want their wishes (e.g about care and support and their desire to refuse treatment in some circumstances) to be known to others. As an additional safeguard, the Act requires an Independent Mental Capacity Advocate (IMCA) to be appointed to assist those who have nobody else to help them or represent their best interests.

Figure 23 – Independent mental capacity advocacy is designed to give people a 'voice' in situations where they may feel overwhelmed.

See also – Advocacy; Autonomy; Mental Health Act 2007.

Mental Health Act 2007

The Mental Health Act 2007 updated the Mental Health Act 1983 and the Mental Capacity Act 2005, which were the main pieces of law affecting the treatment of adults experiencing serious mental disorders in England and Wales.

The Mental Health Act 2007 seeks to safeguard the interests of adults who are vulnerable because of their mental health problems by ensuring that they can be monitored in the community by mental health and social care practitioners and admitted to hospital if they don't comply with treatment. In addition, the 2007 Act:

- introduced Community Treatment Orders, giving approved practitioners the power to bring a person back into hospital for treatment if they stop complying with their treatment (e.g won't take medication) in the community
- ensured that a person cannot be detained in hospital unless 'appropriate treatment' is available for them.
- broadened the role of non-medical mental health practitioners (e.g registered nurses and occupational therapists in particular) so that they could also take on primary responsibility for a person's care and treatment.
- created the role of Approved Mental Health Practitioner so that all registered healthcare practitioners (as well as qualified social workers) could undertake Mental Health Act 1983 (as amended) assessments. These occur before a person can be detained against their will in a psychiatric hospital or unit.
- Gave relatives and civil partners of people admitted to hospital more rights – particularly to be identified as the person's 'nearest relative' for appeal purposes when detention is disputed.

The Mental Health Act 2007 extended the rights of people to appeal against detention and treatment in hospital, introduced the right to be supported by an independent mental health advocate and extended the person's rights to refuse and appeal against electro-convulsive therapy (ECT) treatment.

See also – Autonomy; Legislation; Mental Capacity Act 2005.

Multi-agency working

Multi-agency working refers to collaboration between different health and social care agencies or organisations.

Collaborations between health and social care agencies usually occur where an individual has complex needs that require input from several different professionals or practitioners working for different agencies. For example, an NHS learning disabilities team may collaborate with a housing association and a local authority social work team to meet the complex needs of a person with autism living in supported accommodation in the community.

In some cases, agencies that are part of another sector, such as the police or probation service from the criminal justice sector or education professionals representing a nursery, school, college or university, may also become involved in multi-agency working to promote an individual's development or safeguard their (or other peoples') interests.

Multi-agency working aims to ensure that service provision is planned, coordinated, holistic and more cost-effective. It depends on good communication, effective leadership and a clear understanding of the roles and responsibilities of the different professionals involved. Problems can occur in situations where one or more of these requirements are missing or neglected. In these circumstances gaps in service provision can occur leading to safeguarding issues and ineffective support for the individuals whose needs are not being met.

See also – Healthcare professionals; Multi-disciplinary team; Social care professionals; Voluntary sector workers.

Multi-disciplinary team

A multi-disciplinary team consists of health and/or social care professionals from different backgrounds or care disciplines (nursing, social work, medicine, occupational therapy, for example) who are employed by the same organisation to perform different though complementary work roles within a care team.

Most health and social care services are delivered by care teams so multidisciplinary teams are very common in health and social care settings. They provide a way of pooling resources and expertise and are an efficient means of reducing duplication or overlap of service provision. Effective multidisciplinary teams should be able to provide a comprehensive range of care that meets the complex needs of the individuals referred to them. Where this happens, an individual should receive holistic care that meets their needs more effectively.

Figure 24 – Multi-disciplinary teams comprise a variety of different care practitioners

See also – Education professionals; Healthcare professionals; Multi-agency working; Social care professionals; Voluntary sector workers.

HEALTH AND SOCIAL CARE

National Eligibility Criteria (Care Act 2014)

The Care Act (2014) was introduced to modernise a range of outdated social care legislation in the United Kingdom. A key part of the 2014 Act was the introduction of National Eligibility Criteria that must be used to determine whether an individual is entitled to social care and support from their local authority.

An individual who applies for local authority care and support will have their needs assessed by a local authority assessor (typically a social worker) against three criteria:

1. *Are a person's needs due to a physical or mental impairment or illness?*
   This includes conditions such as physical, mental, sensory, learning or cognitive disabilities or illnesses, brain injuries and substance misuse.
2. *If the person does have needs caused by physical or mental impairment or illness:*
   It should then be considered whether they are unable to achieve two or more of the following outcomes:
   - Managing and maintaining nutrition
   - Maintaining personal hygiene
   - Managing toilet needs
   - Being appropriately clothed
   - Being able to make use of the adult's home safely
   - Maintaining a habitable home environment
   - Developing and maintaining family or other personal relationships
   - Accessing and engaging in work, training, education or volunteering
   - Making use of necessary facilities or services in the local community including public transport and recreational facilities or services
   - Carrying out any caring responsibilities the adult has for a child

3. *If the person does have needs caused by physical or mental impairment or illness; and is unable to achieve two or more specified outcomes it must be considered whether:*
There is a significant impact on the person's wellbeing as a result of their inability to meet the above outcomes.

A person who is eligible for care and support is entitled to have their needs met by the local authority or by a service provider identified by the local authority. The amount of funding provided by the local authority to pay for care and support will depend on how much income and savings the person has. A financial assessment is carried out once the person's eligibility for care and support is established.

Carers National Eligibility Criteria

The 2014 Act also imposed a duty on local authorities to promote the wellbeing of carers. In particular, carers have a right to a carers assessment to determine whether they themselves need support to provide care for their partner or family member. The local authority has to apply the Carers National Eligibility Criteria to arrive at their decision. These focus on the impact that caring has on the carer. Specifically, when determining carer eligibility, the local authority has to consider the following three conditions:

1. The carer's needs for support arise because they are providing necessary care to an adult.
Carers can be eligible for support whether or not the adult for whom they care has eligible needs. The carer must also be providing 'necessary' care (i.e. activities that the individual requiring support should be able to carry out as part of normal daily life but is unable to do so). If the carer is providing care and support for needs that the adult is capable of meeting themselves, the carer may not be providing 'necessary' care and support.

HEALTH AND SOCIAL CARE

2. As a result of their caring responsibilities, the carer's physical or mental health is either deteriorating or is at risk of doing so or the carer is unable to achieve any one of the following outcomes:

- Carrying out any caring responsibilities the carer has for a child
- Providing care to other persons for whom the carer provides care
- Maintaining a habitable home environment in the carer's home, whether or not this is also the home of the adult needing care
- Managing and maintaining nutrition
- Developing and maintaining family or other personal relationships
- Engaging in work, training, education or volunteering
- Making use of necessary facilities or services in the local community, including recreational facilities or services
- Engaging in recreational activities

3. As a consequence of being unable to achieve these outcomes, there is, or there is likely to be, a significant impact on the carer's wellbeing.

See also – Carers; Social care professionals; Support.

National Framework for NHS Continuing Healthcare

NHS continuing healthcare is free health care services provided outside of hospital settings (usually in nursing homes) for adults with long-term healthcare needs. The important thing to note about continuing healthcare is that, once an individual's needs have been assessed, recipients do not have to pay for the care and support they receive. This is inp contrast to social care and support which is means-tested (see *National Eligibility Criteria*) and can be expensive.

A person will only be given continuing healthcare funding and support after they have undergone a comprehensive multi-disciplinary assessment of their needs. This can include general health assessments as well as specialist dementia, mental health, mobility and other assessments. The assessor(s) must agree that an individual has a complex medical condition and a 'primary health need' for ongoing care and support. A person who 'fails' the assessment can appeal if they believe the correct processes were not followed or that the eligibility criteria have been applied incorrectly. Funding can be withdrawn if a subsequent reassessment shows the person's needs have changed.

Continuing health care services are commissioned, and payments administered, by Clinical Commissioning Groups in England. The growing population of older people with complex and continuing health care needs, increasing care costs and reductions in NHS budgets has placed a great deal of pressure on CCGs in respect of continuing healthcare provision.

See also – National Eligibility Criteria (Care Act 2014); Common Assessment Framework (CAF).

NHS Patient Experience Framework

NHS organisations and practitioners want to deliver high quality services in ways that patients / services users find most helpful. This isn't an easy thing to do as the NHS is a very large healthcare system employing 1.3 million people in a wide range of healthcare settings throughout the United Kingdom. However, the NHS Patient Experience Framework has been developed and is used to measure patient experience across the NHS. The Framework outlines a number of important elements of patient experience with the NHS including:

- **Respect for patient-centred values, preferences, and expressed needs,** including: cultural issues; the dignity, privacy and independence of patients and service users; an awareness of quality-of-life issues; and shared decision making;
- **Coordination and integration of care** across the health and social care system;
- **Information, communication, and education** on clinical status, progress, prognosis, and processes of care in order to facilitate autonomy, self-care and health promotion;
- **Physical comfort** including pain management, help with activities of daily living, and clean and comfortable surroundings;
- **Emotional support** and alleviation of fear and anxiety about such issues as clinical status, prognosis, and the impact of illness on patients, their families and their finances;
- **Welcoming the involvement of family and friends,** on whom patients and service users rely, in decision-making and demonstrating awareness and accommodation of their needs as care-givers;
- **Transition and continuity** as regards information that will help patients care for themselves away from a clinical setting, and coordination, planning, and support to ease transitions;

- **Access to care** with attention for example, to time spent waiting for admission or time between admission and placement in a room in an in-patient setting, and waiting time for an appointment or visit in the out-patient, primary care or social care setting.

NHS organisations use patient feedback questionnaires and surveys to ask about and monitor peoples' experiences of using services. By asking people about the areas listed in the Framework, organisations can generate evidence that is useful to themselves as an organisation and to the NHS as a whole. This evidence-based can then be used to make improvements in the areas that patients and their relatives say matter most to them.

See also – Adult Social Care Outcomes Framework; Health Action Plan; Common Assessment Framework (CAF).

Observation skills

Observation of an individual's physical and mental state is an important area of practice in healthcare settings. Healthcare professionals make an important distinction between 'signs' and 'symptoms' of illness and disease. A 'sign' is an objective indication of a medical or health issue that can be detected by the professional or the patient either through direct visual observation or by carrying out a test (e.g a blood test or blood pressure reading). By contrast, a 'symptom', such as an ache, pain or tingling sensation, is a subjective indicator of a possible health problem that can only be experienced or felt by the patient themselves. Healthcare professionals are usually interested in patterns of signs and symptoms as particular combinations may indicate a particular condition or disease.

"For it may safely be said, not that the habit of ready and correct observation will by itself make us useful nurses, but that without it we shall be useless with all our devotion." - Florence Nightingale

Figure 25 – The value of careful patient observation was recognised by Florence Nightingale, a pioneer of modern nursing care.

Healthcare professionals acquire clinical observation skills during their initial training but continue to develop and refine them throughout their careers.

The main ways observation skills are used in health care settings include:

- *Initial assessment of an individual's physical health and mental state*
  A practitioner may note how a person looks, their physical size and shape, whether they have any external, visible signs of illness, injury, pain or disability and also how they relate and respond (are they nervous, aggressive, despondent or inappropriately happy?) when interacting. The practitioner's observations provide an important baseline and inform their first impressions of the person. Remember that the practitioner is looking for patterns or combinations of signs and symptoms to help them work out, and perhaps diagnose, the person's health problems. Their observations provide information that they will combine with the person's own account of what's wrong as well as with any other information available to them (such as reports from other practitioners or test results, for example).

- *Observing changes in an individual's condition*
  If you've been an in-patient in hospital you will probably have had your 'obs' or observations taken on a fairly regular basis by one of the nursing staff. Typically, this involves recording blood pressure, pulse and respirations and writing the results on a chart. These observations provide an indication of underlying physical health and can provide an early warning that medical attention may be required. Additionally, nurses (and care staff in other settings) also tend to monitor the people they are caring for on a constant basis in case there are unexpected changes in a person's physical state. Noticing whether a person is pale, breathing in an unusual way, is unusually sleepy or looks to be in pain can be important indicators that something has changed and needs investigating quickly.

Regular, formal observations are a feature of many different types of health care settings and are critical in achieving safe standards of care practice.

- *Monitoring an individual's response to care and treatment*
  Nursing and other clinical observations tend to be carried out in health care settings after a person has undergone any kind of treatment (including taking medication) or physical intervention. Observing for sudden or unexpected changes in a person's physical health state or for the signs of medication side-effects can be very important at these times. It can also important to note whether, and if so how well, the person has responded to the care and treatment they have received.

- *Monitoring a child's growth and development*
  Pre-school, nursery, paediatric nursing, children's social workers and early years staff tend to have specific training in observing the pattern of children's growth and development. Observation of a child's behaviour, their relationships and play, their physical, social and communication skills (verbal and non-verbal) as well as the way they relate to others provides information about their stage and pattern of development and can also alert staff to developmental delays or safeguarding issues.

- *Monitoring of behaviour and social skills*
  Nurses, allied health professionals and support staff working in learning disabilities, mental health, dementia and early years settings are likely to observe and report on the behaviour and social skills of the people they care for and support. This may be because the people in question experience difficulties in controlling their behaviour or expressing themselves or because these are issues that they are working on as part of their care and treatment.

See also – Communication skills; 6Cs.

Personalised care

The term personalised care is often used as a synonym for individualised care. That is, care that is specifically planned to meet an individual's particular needs and which is delivered in ways that meet that person's wishes and preferences.

Personalised care can be contrasted with approaches to care and treatment that focused on care routines or techniques that are applied to all patients or service users in a care setting regardless of their individual needs. For example, in some long-stay hospitals and nursing homes in the past, all residents / patients would have had their hair washed and been given a bath one after another. A tick or date would then be placed against each resident / patient's name in the so-called 'Bath book' to confirm that this task had been completed. This type of task-focused, conveyor-belt care does not focus on an individual's needs, is impersonal rather than personalised and is now seen as poor practice in contemporary health and social care settings.

Personalised care arguably has its roots in the work of Carl Rodgers, a humanistic psychologist, who introduced the concept of person-centred counselling. When applied to care provision, the person-centred approach aims to acknowledge the whole person (i.e is holistic), sees the person rather than their problems or the service being provided as the primary focus and seeks to support rather than disempower the individual. Health and social care workers seeking to provide personalised care need to consider questions such as:

- What is important to this person?
- How can I/we best support this person?

- How does this person prefer / wish their care and support needs to be met?

Finding out about and being responsive to the individual, respecting the individual's values, rights and preferences and promoting choice and control are all important features of personalised care.

Figure 26 – Individual needs are always at the centre of personalized care.

See also – Autonomy; Care values; Personalisation

Personalisation

According to the Department of Health, personalisation means that "every person who receives support, whether provided by statutory services or funded by themselves, will have choice and control over the shape of that support in all care settings" (DOH, 2007).

Personalisation has its origins in the independent living campaigns of the 1970s disability movement. Disability campaigners at the time advocated a social model of disability based on the values of empowerment and choice. The disability movement resisted institutional living and the controlling 'expertise of professional practitioners such as doctors, nurses and social workers, for example. Disability movement critics felt that recipients of care were treated as passive and were made to fit in with existing services. Independent living required much more personalised provision, ideally chosen by the individual. As a result, disability services have gradually moved away from a care-based approach to a support-based style of provision in which the individual has much greater control and choice in relation to their support and the way(s) it is provided. As a fundamental principle underpinning this change in approach, personalisation guides health and social care practitioners to find ways of ensuring that the person with support needs has as much choice and control over their support as they want or are able to accept.

The Social Care Institute of Excellence (SCIE, 2010) captures much of the debate about, and goals of, personalisation when it suggests that in practice it means:

- tailoring support to individual needs
- ensuring people have access to information, advocacy and support to make informed decisions

- finding new ways of collaborative working so that people can be actively engaged in the design, delivery and evaluation of services
- having leadership and organisational systems that enable staff to work in person-centred ways
- embedding intervention, reablement and prevention
- ensuring a 'total system response' whereby all citizens have access to universal community services and resources.

In effect this means that personalisation has required health and social care service providers to shift the way they think about their role and the strategies they've previously used to provide services. In particular, they must now view individual need and ways of meeting them from the perspective of the service user. In the past, services were created and made available and people were referred to them assuming that there would be a match between service provision and user need. If not, the individual's needs would remain unmet, or perhaps be only partially met. With the introduction of personalisation, health and social care providers now have a responsibility to find, or create / co-produce, services that work best for the person. Changes to the way in which services are funded have been used to facilitate this shift in focus and power away from service providers to service users. Funding strategies such as self-directed support, personal budgets and direct payments to service users are all designed to facilitate the personalisation agenda. Service users eligible for these forms of funding are now in a position to commission their own packages of care and support.

Personalisation is generally seen as a progressive development that, in moving power away from service providers to service users, provides people with a more appropriate, individualised and flexible way of obtaining the types of care and support they want. However, critics of personalisation argue that it:

ABC GUIDE MEETING INDIVIDUAL CARE AND SUPPORT NEEDS

- is overly-individualistic and a threat to the collective provision of care and support services.
- can lead to greater inequality in access to services as not everybody wants or is able to take responsibility for commissioning or managing their own care and support.
- has been, or is being, used as a way of creating a privatised market in care services that undermines public sector (e.g local authority and NHS) provision.
- results in the costs of, and responsibility for, service provision being shifted to service users who find themselves with sources of funding (e.g personal budgets) that are often insufficient to meet their particular care and support needs.

Figure 27 – Personalisation aims to ensure people have choice and control over their own care and support.

See also – Autonomy; Personalised care.
References
Department of Health (2007), *Putting people first: A shared vision and commitment to the transformation of adult social care*, DH.
Social Care Institute of Excellence (2010), *Personalisation: A Rough Guide*, SCIE

Principlism

Principlism is a philosophical approach to ethics and decision-making - a framework of principles - that aims to help those faced with the task of making ethical decisions in difficult clinical circumstances. Principlists, such as Beauchamp and Childress (2008), argue that four key ethical principles are compatible with most societal, individual or religious belief systems and, in combination, can be successfully applied to ethical dilemmas and decision-making situations in health and social care settings. These principles are:

- *Autonomy* – this principle refers to promoting and respecting an individual's freewill or 'agency'. Health and social care professionals have a duty to support all service users to be as autonomous as possible. In particular, people who have mental capacity should always be encouraged and enabled to exercise their autonomy by making their own decisions about the care and treatment they receive.
- *Beneficence* – in short, this principle can be summed up in the phrase 'try to do some good'. This should be the goal of all health and social care practitioners. Beneficence is closely linked to having a 'duty of care' which imposes a responsibility on health and social care workers to always prioritise and act in the best interests of the individual they are caring for or supporting.
- *Non-maleficence* – this ethical principle guides health and social care practitioners 'to do no harm'. It could be seen as the other side of the beneficence coin. However, it is a little more than this. Health and social care practitioners usually do have the best intentions of their patients / service users in mind. However, there may be situations where a treatment or intervention has a number of possible side-effects or is a high risk. Should they go ahead just because they'd like to help the person? Non-maleficence guides the practitioner to weight up

the possible costs as well as the benefits of treating someone or intervening in a person's life. If there is a high risk of harm or if the balance is not in favour of a good outcome, they may be at risk of doing more harm than good.
- *Justice* – this principle refers to the goal of trying to distribute the benefits and burdens of what health and social care professionals in a socially just way. That is, in ways that benefit as many people as possible or which are morally fair and respectful of each person's right to equality.

Principlists argue that whilst each of these four principles are important and help people to think, act and make decisions in a more ethical way, it is the use of the principles in combination that is most valuable. Principlism claims to be a unified moral approach in which each principle strengthens, supports and is balanced by the other principles. Principlism is well known and widely used in the health and social care sector and does seem to provide a useful philosophical / moral framework for guiding thinking and decision-making in what can be very difficult situations.

See also – Autonomy; Care values; Consequentialism; Deontology; Virtue ethics.

References
Beauchamp, T.L and Childress, J.F. (2008), *Principles of Biomedical Ethics, 6th Edition*. Oxford: Oxford University Press, 2008.

Resilience

Resilience is a psychological concept associated with positive psychology. It refers to an individual's ability to draw on and apply the skills, abilities and knowledge they have acquired through education and experience to cope with and tackle the problems they face.

Definitions of resilience are wide and varied. Masten (2001:228) argues that 'resilience refers to a class of phenomenon characterised by good outcomes in spite of serious threats to adaptation or development'. Carr (2004:300) says something similar in suggesting that resilience is 'the capacity to withstand exceptional stresses and demands without developing stress-related problems'.

Resilience is often seen as the other side of the coin to vulnerability. However, it isn't just a static quality that a person has or hasn't got. Beardslee (1989:267) acknowledges the way behaviours and thinking patters interact to produce resilience when defining it as 'unusually good adaptation in the face of severe stress'. Resilience is now most closely associated with the strengths-based approach to health and social care practice.

Figure 28 – Resilience is about getting up again and taking the next step despite the obstacles and difficulties you have to overcome to do so.

The concept of resilience has become more important in health and social care as practitioners have moved away from a 'needs-led' and problem-focused approach to care and support. Recovery-based approaches that focus on an individual's strengths and abilities rather than on their perceived deficits and problems focuses attention on the positive qualities and capacities a person has for dealing with health, psychological and social issues that are affecting their quality of life and ability to cope. This is where resilience comes in!

Health and social care workers who adopt a resilience perspective encourage / motivate and support the people they work with to draw on the range of personal resources available to them in order to address their problems. These include the person's skills, abilities and knowledge as well as their social network (family, friendships and wider relationships). Realising that they have personal resources that can be used to improve their situation and that there are other sources of support (family, friends, neighbours) is a first step in using resilience. Developing new skills and trying out new experiences can also help people to strengthen and develop themselves in a positive, problem-solving way. This is more active and empowering than waiting for health and social care 'experts' to come up with a 'silver bullet' solution or treatment that will solve a person's difficulties. However, a resilience approach doesn't mean that an individual must take on sole responsibility for resolving their difficulties. It is better practice for health and social care workers to promote resilience through a partnership approach that:

- Focuses on wellness, quality of life and recovery rather than illness.
- Recognises each person's individuality.
- Acknowledges the reality and impact of an individual's health problems or social care needs but doesn't see this as a reason to stop the person getting on with their life.

- Promotes and maintains a sense of hope and the expectation that the person can continue to enjoy, or regain, a good quality of life.

The resilience approach is now quite widely accepted and used in health and social care settings – especially where trauma, rehabilitation and recovery are important issues. However, the resilience approach is not above criticism. Those who do have reservations about it argue that:

- The resilience approach, and the idea that everyone can develop resilience, doesn't always acknowledge the extent to which a person's illness or life trauma really can undermine an individual's capacity to cope and be independent.
- It can be 'victim-blaming'. For example, are people who have little resilience not taking responsibility to getting better or improve their circumstances? Should they just 'try harder'? Saying that a person 'lacks resilience' can sometimes involve blaming them when, in fact, the person lacks support – which is not their fault!

See also – Attachment; Ethical issues; Empathy.

References
Beardslee, W.R. (1989), 'The role of self-understanding in resilient individuals: The development of a perspective', *American Journal of Orthopsychiatry*, 59 (1989), pp.266-278.
Carr, A. (2004), *Positive Psychology: The Psychology of Happiness and Human Strengths*, Brunner-Routledge.
Masten, A.S. (2001), 'Ordinary Magic: Resilience processes in development', American Psychologist, 56 (2001), pp.227-238.

Risk

Risk refers to the chance or likelihood that a person may be harmed by a hazard.

This definition of risk begs the question – what is a 'hazard'? A hazard is anything that could potentially cause harm or have an adverse impact on a person's health, development or wellbeing. A person's life can never be made risk free. We all face hazards that are outside of our control (such as 'natural disasters', inheriting 'faulty' genes, virus infections, for example) as well as a wide range of human-made hazards (traffic, drinking excess alcohol, environmental pollution, for example) on a daily basis. The risk factors that each person faces – whether biological, psychosocial or environmental in origin – increase the likelihood that they will experience negative health or development outcomes. However, the existence of a potentially bewildering range of hazards in everyday life doesn't preoccupy health and social care workers too much. What is important is that they develop and apply risk assessment and risk management skills in their work with service users (and each other).

Risk assessment
Risk assessment is the process of identifying hazards and then evaluating the likelihood of a hazard actually causing harm. It is now a key feature of care practice for all health and social care workers. In practice, health and social care workers focus on assessing two types of risk:

- The risks a person poses to others (dangerousness)
- The risks a person is subject to (vulnerability)

In the majority of cases, health and social care workers are more likely to find themselves focusing on safeguarding and health and safety issues rather than the risks a person may pose to others. This is more a feature of mental health and some learning disabilities settings but does need to be taken seriously where it is an issue.

Hazards in care settings
Hazards in the physical environment of care settings include:

- *Faulty electrical appliances*, switches, overloaded sockets, frayed flexes and power surges can all lead to fires, burns and electrical shocks, for example
- *Faulty gas appliances and gas leaks* can lead to fires, explosions, breathing difficulties, unconsciousness and asphyxiation
- *Water leaks* result in wet floors, walls and carpets as well as rotten floorboards. All of these things cause accidents and injuries if people slip or trip. If there is contact between water and electricity there is also a danger of electrocution.
- *Kitchen hazards* include sharp knives, cooking appliances, pot handles hanging over edge of cooker, slippery floors, contaminated food.
- *Living room and/ bedroom hazards* include worn or badly fitted carpets, loose rugs, poorly placed furniture, floor length curtains, clothes or bed linen left on the floor, trailing flexes, poor lighting, electrical appliances, fires without guards
- *Bathroom hazards* include hot water, wet slippery surfaces and floors, electrical items near water
- *Stairs* are hazardous if they lack hand rails, are steep or have poorly fitted, loose carpets.

Examples of care equipment hazards include:
- mobility aids that are the wrong size or which do not work properly
- faulty or damaged lifting equipment
- brakes and hydraulics on beds that do not work properly

- computer display screens and keyboards that are badly located, poorly serviced or over-used
- blades and syringe needles that are stored or disposed of incorrectly
- unlabelled, incorrectly labelled or leaking bottles and containers
- old and faulty electrical and gas-fuelled appliances
- excessively full or faulty waste disposal equipment

Care practitioners should always check the equipment that they intend to use to ensure it is safe and free of hazards. They should not use equipment that is faulty or which they have not been trained to use. Faulty, unsafe equipment should be reported and removed from the care setting.

The aim of risk assessment is to provide information that can be used to develop risk management strategies. These are ways of practising that reduce or minimise the likelihood of a potential hazard affecting the individual. The Health and Safety Executive has identified five stages of risk assessment (see figures 25 and 26).

HEALTH AND SOCIAL CARE

Figure 29 – The stages of risk assessment

Stage	Key questions	Purpose
1 - Look for hazards	What are the hazards?	To identify all hazards
2 - Assess who may be harmed	Who is at risk?	To evaluate the risk of hazards causing harm
3 - Consider the risk – whether existing precautions are adequate	What needs to be done? Who needs to do what?	To consider risk control measures To identify risk control responsibilities
4 - Document the findings	Can you give a summary of the hazards and risks?	To record all findings and the risk control plan.
5 - Review the assessment and revise if necessary	Is the risk controlled? Are further controls needed?	To monitor and maintain an accurate and up-to-date risk control system.

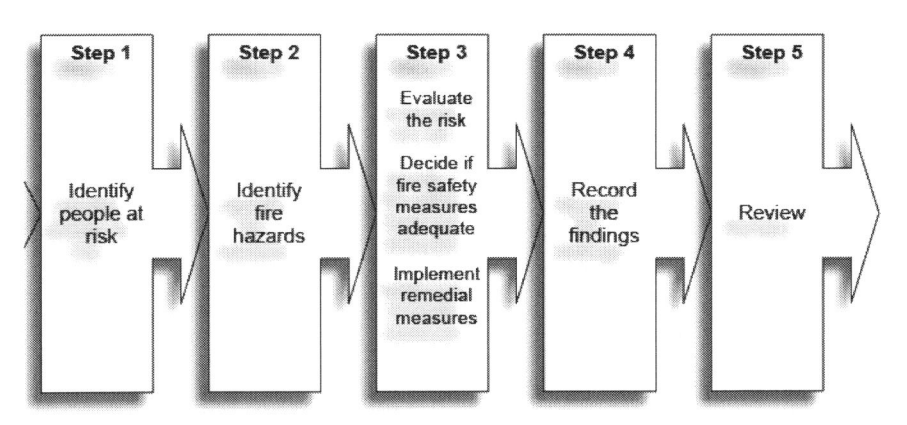

Step 1: Identify people at risk
Step 2: Identify fire hazards
Step 3: Evaluate the risk. Decide if fire safety measures adequate. Implement remedial measures
Step 4: Record the findings
Step 5: Review

Figure 30 – A diagram illustrating the 5 steps to take in carrying out a risk assessment related to fire hazards in a care home.

ABC GUIDE MEETING INDIVIDUAL CARE AND SUPPORT NEEDS

The Management of Health and Safety at Work Regulations (1999) place a legal duty on employers to carry out risk assessments in order to ensure a safe and healthy workplace. The risk assessments that are produced should clearly identify:

- the potential hazards and risks to the health, safety and security of employees and others in the workplace
- any preventive and protective measures that are needed to minimise risk and improve health and safety.

Care practitioners can also carry out their own ongoing risk assessments in their everyday work. Basically this involves:

- being alert to possible hazards
- understanding the risks associated with each hazard
- reporting any health, safety or security concerns that are identified.

See also – Ethical issues.

HEALTH AND SOCIAL CARE

6Cs

The 6Cs are a set of care values associated through national care policy developments designed to improve the quality of care provision and service delivery throughout the NHS. The policy identifying and introducing the 6Cs followed notable failures in care provision at Winterbourne View hospital for people with learning disabilities and Mid Staffordshire NHS Trust.

Figure 31 – The 6Cs of care

Care value	What does it mean?
Care	Every health and social care practitioner should be committed to providing a genuinely caring service that meets the individual needs of the person they are working with.
Compassion	This refers to the use of empathy and ensuring that all service users are treated with respect and dignity. Service users should feel that the care workers who support them are doing so in a compassionate way.
Competence	Care workers should always understand an individual's needs and have the knowledge and professional skills and expertise to deliver effective care.

Care value	What does it mean?
Communication	Effective communication skills are needed for team working and for carefully listening and responding appropriately to service users and those who support them.
Courage	This refers to having the desire to do the right thing for each service user and then taking appropriate action to do this in practice. It also involves being open to innovative ideas and having a willingness to embrace change.
Commitment	Health and social care workers should continually support individuals to the best of their abilities and should always be trying to improve care for and the experiences of the people they work with. This commitment to people and standards is vital in providing service users with high quality care.

See also – Care values; Communication skills; Empathy

References
Compassion in Practice

Social care commissioning

Social care services refer to non-medical forms of support and assistance provided to people with social, emotional, practical and financial support needs. Social care services are commissioned (bought) in two main ways:

- Local authorities are responsible for commissioning social care (including safeguarding) services to meet the identified needs of their local populations. Each local authority has a legal or statutory responsibilities to provide certain services to adults and children with care and support needs. A local authority needs to decide how to provide assessment and direct care services. They tend to commission assessment services from their own social services department and then make agreements with other private and voluntary sector organisations to provide direct support services to meet individual's identified needs as part of a care and support 'package'.

- The introduction of personalisation as a strategy for delivering adult social care has led to a change in the way adult social care is commissioned for some people with identified needs. The goal of personalisation is to ensure that an individual has greater choice and control over services provided for them. The Health and Social Care Act 2001 placed a mandatory duty on local authorities to offer direct payments to all eligible people requesting one. Direct payments allow people to commission some or all of they require themselves. Data produced by Skills for Care (2016) indicates that approximately 65 000 people now use direct payments to commission their own support services.

See also – Healthcare commissioning organisations; National Eligibility Criteria (Care Act 2014); Social Care professionals; Support;

References
Skills for Care (2016), *The size and structure of the adult social care sector and workforce in England, 2016,* Skills for Care

Social care workers

Social care workers are those employed in public, private and voluntary sector services to provide forms of social work and non-medical social support for people with identified personal, care and support needs. Some social care workers, such as social workers and occupational therapists, are registered practitioners (see HCPC). There are also many social care roles being carried out by unregistered workers who have varying levels of training and a range of different types of qualification.

Approximately two thirds of the social care workforce are employed in the voluntary and private sectors. The other third is employed within the statutory or public sector, mainly by local authorities, delivering children's and adult social care services.

Data on the social care workforce is collected and analysed by Skills for Care, the national workforce organization for adult social care in England. Data is collected through the organisation's National Minimum Data Set (NMDS-SC). Using this data, it's 2016 report on the social care workforce stated that:

- the number of adult social care jobs in England as at 2015 was estimated to be 1.55 million. An increase of 1% and 12,500 jobs since 2014.
- The number of people doing these jobs was estimated at 1.43 million.
- The number of full-time equivalent jobs was estimated at 1.11 million.
- An estimated 19,300 organisations spread across 40,100 care providing locations were involved in providing or organising adult social care in England
- Around 235,000 adults, older people and carers received direct payments from council social services departments. It is

estimated that approximately 65,000 direct payment recipients employ their own staff.
- Since 2009, the workforce continued to shift away from local authority jobs (-33% and -60,000 jobs) and towards independent sector jobs (+25% and 245,000 jobs).

Social care workers are employed in a range of care settings including the community, hospitals, health centres, education and advice centres and people's homes. Like healthcare professionals, social care workers typically work in teams, some multi-disciplinary, and may also be involved in multi-agency working (with health, housing, education, legal and advice / advocacy services) to support individuals with complex or extensive care and support needs.

In general, adult social care workers support:
- older people
- people with physical disabilities
- people with learning disabilities
- people experiencing mental health problems.

Other more specific groups who are seen as vulnerable and in need of social care and support include:
- people with substance misuse problems
- people with HIV / AIDS
- asylum seekers and refugees
- homeless people
- ex-offenders

Some people who receive adult social care fall into more than one of the service user groups listed above.

See also – Carers; Health and Care Professions Council (HCPC); Healthcare professionals.

Support

The concept of 'support' is generally understood to be a psychosocial feature of relationships. People give and receive support within relationships and also have a felt, or subjective, sense of whether their relationship(s) with another person is supportive. The support that people offer to, and receive from, each other can be emotional (e.g nurturance), tangible (e.g financial assistance), informational (e.g advice), based on companionship (e.g a sense of belonging) or more intangible (e.g. personal connection).

Health and social care workers are encouraged to develop and maintain supportive relationships with patients/service users. Part of the reason for this is that being supportive keeps the person engaged and involved in the relationship but it also contributes to their health and wellbeing. Leach (2015), for example, suggests social support has beneficial effects on mental health and wellbeing. He describes the social support that people provide for each other as "the everyday help and reassurance that friends, relatives, colleagues and others give each other throughout their lives. It can both protect against mental distress and help people cope with the effects of mental health problems".

Figure 32 – Support is often seen as the emotional part of a helping relationship.

When support is contrasted with 'care' it is usually seen as being less structured, deliberate or technical (e.g social support v medical care). It tends to be seen as a relationship-based form of assistance typically provided by non-professionals. For example, when a care practitioner is assessing whether a person has sufficient 'social support' they are thinking about whether there is a network of friends, family and acquaintances (such as neighbours and work colleagues) surrounding the person. This kind of informal social support is important for both physical and mental health because lack of social support is associated with social isolation and feelings of loneliness. Even when a person has a social network they can still feel lonely if those relationships are unsupportive or actually detrimental to their well-being. Social support is not just a matter of how many people you know but of how supportive they actually are towards you.

Social scientists and health and social care practitioners became more interested in the role of social support in society, and its impact on health and wellbeing, in the 1980s. Clarifying both the nature of social support and its benefits, Albrecht and Adelman (1987) argued that there are 3 main aspects to social support interactions:

- they meet a need for human contact, which involves making sense of one's life and the events that occur within it
- supportive interactions help reduce feelings of uncertainty, both about the situation a person finds themselves in and about their relationship with the other person. This leads to the person having a greater sense of control over their life and over the stressful conditions that might adversely affect them
- social support takes place within a structure of connected and reciprocal relationships, some strong, some weak, in which help is given and received.

HEALTH AND SOCIAL CARE

Turner and Brown (2010) have since referred to social support as a multidimensional construct comprising:
- Perceived support – knowing support is available if needed
- Structural support – the presence of social ties and a network that can be used as a resource
- Received support – the actual provision of helpful information or practical assistance provided by others.

Health and social care practitioners now recognise that social support helps people to feel (and be) connected with each other, gives people a valued identity and enables people to deal with stressful conditions more effectively. In addition to assessing the extent to which a person has social support available to them, care practitioners will often develop care and treatment plans based around the provision of social support and which aim to introduce, develop or extend the social support a person has available to them. There are many ways of doing this but at the heart of all of them is connecting a person to others through positive, nurturing relationships.

Figure 33 – The goal of support is to connect people through nurturing relationships.

See also – Care.

References
Albrecht, T. and Adelman, M. (1987), *Communicating social support*, Sage
Turner, R. and Brown, R. (2010), 'Social Support and mental health', in T.Scheid and T.Brown (eds) *A Handbook for the Study of Mental Health: Social Contexts, Theories and Systems*, Cambridge University Press
Leach, J (2015) *Improving mental health through social support*, JKP

Triangle of Care

The Triangle of Care is an approach to care that seeks to ensure that service users, their carers / relatives and health and social care staff work together as part of a 'therapeutic alliance'. This is seen to promote safety, support recovery and sustain wellbeing more effectively. The Triangle of Care was developed as a way of improving practice in mental health settings. It has now been extended to dementia care practice and is recognised as a feature of good care practice.

The Triangle of Care approach was developed to overcome a model of mental health care practice that excluded carers at important points. For example, not consulting or obtaining information from carers during mental health assessments can result in vital information about a person's current or recent mental state being missed. Similarly, creating care and support plans that do not include carers or take account of their expert role and experience in supporting their relative can result in impractical and unrealistic plans that do not succeed in practice. The Triangle of Care encourages everyone involved in supporting an individual to act in their best interests, to receive support themselves where necessary and to be fully informed about developments or changes in care plans or treatment

The benefits of the Triangle of Care model include:

- recognition for the carer.
- others appreciate the carer's unique knowledge about the person they care for.
- emotional and practical support – enabling carers to have a life of their own alongside their caring role.
- helping carers to feel part of a team and less isolated.
- creating a more helpful, supportive relationship with carers.
- giving carers and service users realistic expectations.

- ensuring staff have information about service users' moods, behaviours and the best way to interact with them.

The Triangle of Care brings together many years of research with carers into what they feel will benefit them when involved with mental health services. Carers are often the only constant in the service user's mental health care journey. They are there when crisis occurs, when the person is well and when that person needs support with day-to-day activities. They often understand the service user's needs and condition extremely well and as such are a vital partner in care. The goal of the Triangle of Care is to promote better care and support for service users and a level of support and involvement for carers that will help them to maintain or improve their own wellbeing.

See also – Carers; Empathy; Healthcare professionals; Resilience; Social care professionals

Virtue ethics

Virtue ethics is a philosophical approach to ethics that focuses on the character and qualities of the person rather than on their actions or the consequences of the decisions they make. From this perspective, a virtuous person will always do the right thing.

Virtue ethics considers the rightness or wrongness of individual actions whilst also offering guidance on the sort of characteristics and behaviours a good person will seek to develop. From a virtue ethics perspective:

- An action is only right if it is an action that a virtuous person would carry out in the same circumstances.
- A virtuous person is a person who acts virtuously
- A person acts virtuously if they "possess and live the virtues"
- A virtue is a moral characteristic that a person needs to live well.

So what 'virtues' should a person try to develop? In general virtue ethics suggests the following principles should be part of our character (who we are) and guide our behaviour (what we do):

- Justice – this requires us to treat all people fairly and equally
- Fidelity – this requires that we treat people close to us with special care
- Self-care – this suggests that we have a unique responsibility to care for ourselves physically and emotionally
- Prudence – this suggests that the prudent person should seek opportunities to acquire more of the other three virtues

Some of the strengths of the virtue ethics approach is that it focuses on the person, what it means to be human and includes the whole of a person's life. In this sense the character of an individual is a core part of their effectiveness as a health and social care worker. This implies that certain character features (e.g 'being caring') are needed to become an effective practitioner. However, virtue ethics isn't particularly useful in helping practitioners resolve ethical dilemmas. It doesn't provide guidance on how they might approach a difficult situation, for example, beyond encouraging the individual to be the best, most virtuous person they can be. Obviously a virtuous person would always know what to do and would try to do it – but there is no general agreement on what 'being virtuous' entails! It is highly likely that different people would prioritise different virtues and that their preferred 'virtues' would be strongly influenced by their culture and beliefs.

See also – Care values; Confidentiality; Consequentialism; Deontology; Principlism;

HEALTH AND SOCIAL CARE

Voluntary sector workers

People who work for charities and other not-for-profit organisations and agencies can be described as voluntary sector workers.

The voluntary sector is defined by its 'not-for-profit', charitable approach to providing services. This doesn't mean that voluntary sector workers aren't employed or don't get paid. There is, in fact, a distinction between the many unpaid 'volunteers' who provide a range of services and forms of support for free (i.e without being paid) and voluntary sector workers who are employed and paid by voluntary sector organisations / agencies. It is this group who are most accurately described as voluntary sector workers. Macmillan cancer support nurses, for example, are voluntary sector workers because they are both qualified and paid for the work they do.

Figure 34 – Volunteers are an important part of the voluntary sector but are not usually paid or employed by the organisations they work with and support.

Some voluntary sector workers have health or social care qualifications and provide direct care and support services as part of their work roles. Other voluntary sector workers are employed in finance, marketing, management and training roles, within voluntary sector organisations, for example.

See also – Carers; Healthcare professionals; Social Care professionals

Printed in Great Britain
by Amazon